# Reading in the Content Areas: Research for Teachers

Mary M. Dupuis, Editor
Pennsylvania State University

 International Reading Association
800 Barksdale Road, Box 8139, Newark, Delaware 19714

**ERIC**® Clearinghouse on Reading and Communication Skills
National Institute of Education

# INTERNATIONAL READING ASSOCIATION

**Published 1984**
International Reading Association
ERIC Clearinghouse on Reading and Communication Skills
National Institute of Education

**Library of Congress Cataloging in Publication Data**
Main entry under title:

Reading in the content areas: Research for teachers.

Bibliography: p.
1. Reading comprehension—Study and teaching—
Teacher training—Addresses, essays, lectures.
2. Individualized reading instruction—Teacher training—
Addresses, essays, lectures.  3. Study, Method of—
Addresses, essays, lectures.  4. Teachers—Inservice
training.  5. Readers—Curricula.  I. Dupuis, Mary M.
II. International Reading Association.
LB1050.45.R44   1984        428.4'07'1        83-8577
ISBN 0-87207-857-4

# Contents

The International Reading Association attempts, through its publications, to provide a forum for a wide spectrum of opinions on reading. This policy permits divergent viewpoints without assuming the endorsement of the Association.

This publication was prepared with funding from the National Institute of Education, U.S. Department of Education, under contract no. 400-83-0025. Contractors undertaking such projects under government sponsorship are encouraged to express freely their judgment in professional and technical matters. Prior to publication, the manuscript was submitted to the International Reading Association for critical review and determination of professional competency. This publication has met such standards. Points of view or opinions, however, do not necessarily represent the official view or opinions of either the International Reading Association or the National Institute of Education.

# Foreword

Much has been written about reading in the content areas. Numerous books and journals provide countless practical suggestions for content area teachers to aid them in making texts more meaningful for their students. In addition, many suggested strategies are also available to help reading teachers integrate content into their teaching of reading skills. Despite this plethora of information, there exists no comprehensive source delineating actual research in content area reading. This volume fills that gap.

Mary Dupuis, editor of this volume, has organized this work around seven specific content areas: English, foreign language, mathematics, music, physical education, science, and social studies. Six different authors then compiled and described specific research related to each of the seven content areas mentioned above.

Some of the subject areas such as music, physical education, and foreign language have heretofore received little attention from authorities in content area reading. This book will be a much needed resource for these subject areas.

One of the stated purposes for the publication of this volume is to provide a stimulus for needed research in the content areas—particularly research dealing with comprehending neglected subject areas and with ascertaining the effectiveness of certain instructional techniques. With this volume as a base, prospective researchers will have a valuable resource on which to base their studies. Mary Dupuis and her coauthors are to be commended for providing this much needed collection of research on this very important subject.

Jack Cassidy, *President*
International Reading Association
1982-1983

# Preface

The Educational Resources Information Center (ERIC) is a national information system developed by the U.S. Office of Education and now sponsored by the National Institute of Education (NIE). It provides ready access to descriptions of exemplary programs, research and development efforts, and related information useful in developing more effective educational programs.

Through its network of specialized centers or clearinghouses, each of which is responsible for a particular educational area, ERIC acquires, evaluates, abstracts, and indexes current significant information and lists this information in its reference publications.

ERIC/RCS, The ERIC Clearinghouse on Reading and Communication Skills, disseminates educational information related to research, instruction, and personnel preparation at all levels and in all institutions. The scope of interest of the Clearinghouse includes relevant research reports, literature reviews, curriculum guides and descriptions, conference papers, project or program reviews, and other print materials related to all aspects of reading, English, educational journalism, and speech communication.

The ERIC system has already made available—through the ERIC Document Reproduction System—much informative data. However, if the findings of specific educational research are to be intelligible to teachers and applicable to teaching, considerable bodies of data must be re-evaluated, focused, translated, and molded into an essentially different context. Rather than resting at the point of making research reports readily accessible, NIE has directed the separate clearinghouses to work with professional organizations in developing information analysis papers in specific areas within the scope of the clearinghouses.

ERIC is pleased to cooperate with the International Reading Association in making available *Reading in the Content Areas: Research for Teachers.*

Bernard O'Donnell
Director, ERIC/RCS

# Introduction

Mary M. Dupuis
*Pennsylvania State University*

Content area reading has been an area of growing interest and research in the past few years. Reading teachers are becoming aware of their role as resource teacher to content teachers at all grade levels. Because reading teachers can't expect to keep up with research and teaching techniques in every subject, this monograph was developed to provide a handy reference to both research and teaching techniques in the important academic teaching areas.

Reading teachers and supervisors are frequently asked to provide information to content teachers about teaching reading. Perhaps it is better for the reading teacher to provide sources of information and allow the content teacher to do some searching. However it is done, the sources of information on the most recent research in content area reading need to be available. This monograph is such a source.

The research on implementing reading instruction in content areas suggests two major problems. First, content teachers know less than they need to about reading in general and the specific aspects of teaching reading within their own subjects. Second, content teachers often have negative attitudes toward the teaching of reading. Common reactions from content teachers are helplessness and frustration in the face of students who cannot read classroom materials (Dupuis & Askov, 1979; Dupuis et al., 1979). This monograph is aimed at providing sources of information for content teachers to remedy, in part, the first problem. Research and experience both demonstrate that with knowledge come more positive attitudes, hence a partial solution to the second problem.

All content areas are germane to the study of reading. The typical academic areas are included here: English or literature, social studies, science, and mathematics. Foreign language, art, and music are also included, as areas related through the humanities. These are taught not only in the intermediate grades (4-6), but in junior and senior high school. The areas of vocational education and the practical arts (home economics, industrial arts) are omitted only because of the volume of work. These areas would constitute a monograph in themselves. The scope of this monograph, then, is the academic areas, focusing on grades 4-12.

When the team preparing this monograph began its search, the task seemed formidable. Over twenty textbooks are currently published to teach teachers how to deal with reading in content classrooms. These texts run primarily to practical activities which can be used in the classroom. A search through those books for the research base for their activities reveals circular references, but few sources based on research. Perhaps this is not an uncommon situation. Certain techniques come to be accepted as useful, by a kind of "received wisdom" rather than careful research. Our team was concerned to find the research base for particular techniques in specific content areas where that was discoverable, and to point out where research is needed, if none was found.

It was clear from the beginning that many areas of reading are common across all disciplines (Hafner, 1977; Herber, 1978; Shepherd, 1982; Vacca, 1981). Vocabulary and word attack skills are areas identified in all disciplines. Comprehension is seen across disciplines as the key to reading success. However, both vocabulary and comprehension are treated differently in different disciplines. Study skills differ widely between disciplines (Thomas & Robinson, 1982). The reviews which follow assume that all disciplines have concerns with vocabulary and comprehension, but the reviews will deal only with the elements of concern within that discipline. Similarly, while all disciplines deal with some types of study skills, the reviews will deal only with those considered useful in that area. The choices made to include or exclude references are consistent. We are searching for what makes each content area different in its reading demands on students.

The organization of each review is similar. The opening section is a summary or overview of the important research on reading in that content area, showing the major areas of concern and unique features of reading in that area. Following that is a section including skills emphasized in the area and specific teaching strategies for use in that area.

Some areas (science, mathematics, social studies) have extensive bibliographies of research and/or teaching techniques germane to the subject. Mathematics in particular has generated a great deal of research into the reading process specifically geared to mathematical writing. Some research is also available in science and social studies. Research in reading for English has focused on reading literature, with more emphasis on attitude and interest than in the other subjects (Carlson, 1980). Other subject areas (music, physical education and health, foreign language) have not received as much attention from researchers. Hence the research reviews are brief and, in some cases, nonexistent. That is, no research in reading in that content area is available.

The same situation seems to apply in the section on teaching techniques. A large number of references are available in science, mathematics, English, and social studies. Relatively few are found in music and foreign language. Both provide some confusion for subject teachers, because reading has a plural meaning for them. Reading music is a technical problem for music teachers and not germane to this discussion. We are focusing on reading about music in a music class. Similarly, foreign language teachers face the technical problem of teaching students to read the second language. Our concern is with reading in English about the second language or culture. The results of our search in both areas indicate that while some research is available in the technical areas of both subjects, very little has been done with our concerns in content area reading. Hence, the reviews in these subject areas are limited. Clearly, these are areas in need of research and information on effective teaching techniques. The conclusion of each chapter includes both areas of needed research and sources of information for use by teachers in that content area. The review is followed by an annotated bibliography of sources, both books and articles, for reading in that content area.

The Appendix lists an inventory of texts in content area reading. These books are general texts in the area, with different organizational patterns and reading philosophies. A few are referred to in the subject area reviews, insofar as they include material on specific subject areas. The inventory is included for information only.

We present this review of research as an unending process. While the sources listed here are up-to-date as of January 1982, we know that much more becomes available as each month's journals are published. However, this review can provide a reference and starting point for work with content area reading. Our goal is both to provide this reference point and to stimulate research in the areas where it is clearly needed. In addition, we believe teachers, both subject teachers and reading teachers, can help other teachers by sharing their effective teaching techniques with the profession.

## References

Carlson, G.R. *Books and the teenage reader* (2nd rev. ed.). New York: Harper & Row, 1980.

Dupuis, M.M., Askov, E.N., & Lee, J.W. Changing attitudes toward content area reading: The content area reading project. *Journal of Educational Research,* 1979, *73*, 66-74.

Dupuis, M.M., & Askov, E.N. Combining university and school based inservice education in content area reading. In M.C. Kamie and A.J. Moe (Eds.), *Reading research: Studies and applications*, 28th Yearbook of the National Reading Conference. Clemson, South Carolina: National Reading Conference, 1979, 223-227.

Hafner, L.E. *Developmental reading in middle and secondary schools: Foundations, strategies, and skills for teaching.* New York: Macmillan, 1977.

Herber, H.L. *Teaching reading in content areas* (2nd. ed.). Englewood Cliffs, New Jersey: Prentice-Hall, 1978.

Shepherd, D.L. *Comprehensive high school reading methods* (3rd. ed.). Columbus, Ohio: Charles E. Merrill, 1982.

Thomas, E.L., & Robinson, H.A. *Improving reading in every class: A sourcebook for teachers* (3rd ed.). Boston: Allyn and Bacon, 1982.

Vacca, R.T. *Content area reading.* Boston: Little, Brown, 1981.

# Reading in the Content Area of English

Carol T. Fishel
*Pennsylvania State University*

## Overview

Is content area reading in English class a contradiction in terms? Have not reading and writing skills always been in the province of the English teacher? The answers to these questions are not simple. In the early elementary grades, the language arts teacher does assume the primary role in the acquisition of reading and writing skills. However, with the fourth grade, reading for information, enjoyment, and intellectual development increases with scant attention given to the reading process itself. Even in English class, teachers assume that the student who can read is able to efficiently process and learn from a variety of written materials. In recent years, new attention has been directed to reading in English since the development of the process of reading is integral to the development of thinking skills.

A closer examination of English as a content area reveals several unique reading demands. Reading skills are necessary to comprehend selections from a variety of genres as well as expository text and periodicals. Yet unlike other areas in which rewriting text is often used, English demands that each author's style and linguistic choices be preserved. The problem of maintaining the integrity of an author's artistic composition while enabling the young reader to comprehend and appreciate it can be met by application of what has been learned about reading in English class.

An initial look at research in this area will be followed by a discussion of skills and strategies. The conclusions and annotated bibliography may assist the reader in further exploration of this area.

# Research

Research in the past five years has focused on the effects of strategies which facilitate vocabulary development and comprehension for both able and less able readers.

Gipe (1980) investigated the effects of four methods of vocabulary development. For able and less able readers in both third and fifth grades, the context method was significantly better than the other three methods. Learning the words in context seemed to be highly facilitative for using the words in context. A surprising finding was that categorization was not significantly effective in vocabulary learning.

In related studies, Pressley, Levin, and Miller (1981) investigated a keyword strategy of taking a familiar part from a new word, such as *cat* from *catkin*, and forming an image merging the familiar meaning with the obscure meaning. Subjects in all control groups were instructed to use whatever strategy they desired. Keyword subjects in all four studies performed significantly better than did control subjects.

These four experiments seem to indicate that students can be taught efficient strategies for learning new vocabulary. Yet many questions about the efficacy of different strategies for different age groups and reading abilities are to be answered.

In the area of comprehension research in English, most work has been done with short stories, but a small amount of research has involved teaching the structure of the language to facilitate comprehension.

Since connectives are often taught to students who are learning compound and complex sentences, Soltis and Pflaum (1979) investigated the effects of instruction in connectives on the comprehension of seventh and eighth grade innercity subjects.

The experimental treatment involved identification of connectives in text, learning categories of connectives, and completing worksheets with the connectives (for a desired relational meaning). Using both the Standard Test Lessons in Reading and a cloze-like Connectives Test, they found significant differences only on the Connectives Test. The value of the treatment is difficult to ascertain since instruction in one skill usually has little effect on standardized reading tests.

Several comprehension studies have been done with short stories to explore what instructional strategies may facilitate comprehension for both able and less able readers.

Lucking (1976) examined the effects of hierarchically-ordered comprehension questions based on the Bloom-Clegg taxonomy.

In Phase I, students read the short story silently and then wrote the essay. In Phase II, students read the story and were led in an unstructured discussion by untrained teachers. In Phase III, teachers questioned students after reading using hierarchically-ordered questions moving up the Bloom-Clegg Taxonomy. After each phase, student attitudes were assessed and essays were evaluated by the Purves content analysis scheme (1968). At the end of Phase III, subjects exhibited more interpretation in their essays and more positive attitudes than at the end of either Phases I or II. The author believes that the larger amount of interpretation represents the growth of broader meanings above the literal knowledge level.

Again dealing with questioning strategies, Donlan and Singer (1979) investigated the effects of preposed questions on the comprehension of short stories. Using high school subjects the experimenters examined teacher-prepared questions (similar to those used on a Directed Reading Activity), student-preposed questions, and schema based student-preposed questions. Results from a content-based comprehension test indicated the students using self-preposed questions based on the short story schema exhibited the best comprehension. Teacher-prepared questions narrowed comprehension while student-preposed questions tended to be irrelevant and limited comprehension. Awareness of short story structures from general schema questions seemed to be crucial for forming effective questions.

Weisberg examined the question of whether less able readers are poor comprehenders because of reading difficulties or whether able and less able readers exhibit processing differences in using linguistically coded prior knowledge to understand. She investigated fourth grade readers' comprehension of six short stories presented through visual and auditory modes and tested through free and probed recall (Weisberg, 1979). Less able readers recalled significantly less explicit and implicit information and could answer significantly fewer probed questions than could the more able readers. Perhaps the less able readers have difficulty encoding linguistically, or they may have inefficient retrieval strategies. Weisberg believes that the difference in memory for idea units between the able and less able readers— regardless of mode of presentation—supports a general language comprehension deficit in less able readers. One may question whether the comprehension difficulty is general or with more school-based language structures, such as the short story.

In a related study, Aulls and Gelbert (1980) investigated the effects of instructional methods on the literal comprehension of short stories by able and less able readers in the seventh grade. One group received vocabulary training in a game format on words deemed crucial to a literal understanding of plot, theme, and setting. These subjects then used the vocabulary words as a type of advance organizer to predict the story. Group two received identical vocabulary training but the actual silent reading was guided by a compressed speech reading of the story (230-260 wpm). The third group received only the paced reading treatment, and the fourth group read silently. Results indicated that the vocabulary work and paced reading provided optimal results for the more able readers. The paced reading was more effective for less able readers, perhaps because they can shift attention from decoding to meaning.

In the above study, less able readers benefited from an opportunity to both hear and read the story at the same time. In Weisberg's study (1979), reading or hearing alone was found not to be highly facilitative. More investigation of these problems of semantic redundancy should be done to enable the classroom teacher to choose more effective instructional strategies.

In the area of critical comprehension of short stories, an internationally-based study of critical literary skills under the auspices of the International Association for the Evaluation of Educational Achievement revealed that high school students from New Zealand scored highest in comprehension. Part of the study involved having students in ten countries read three internationally acclaimed short stories translated into their own language. Given twenty questions from three categories (form, content, affect), the students were asked to choose the five they considered most critical to the understanding of each story. Findings indicated that the New Zealand students flexibly chose different questions for different stories; such critical flexibility may facilitate comprehension (Guthrie, 1980).

In the area of interest and motivation, Cline and Kretke (1980) studied sustained silent reading with several hundred subjects in three junior high schools. An inventory of reading attitudes showed that sub-jects involved in a three-year sustained silent reading program exhibited significantly more positive attitudes toward reading than did the control subjects. Reading achievement scores on the Stanford Reading Achievement Test revealed no significant differences between the two groups and no interaction of treatment with intellectual capacity.

Since English revolves around reading various literary genres, little readability work has been done in research. Dupuis (1976, 1980) investigated the cloze procedure as a means of predicting students' ability to read short stories. A 48 percent cloze score predicted minimum comprehension. The conclusion reached was that the cloze procedure can be helpful to teachers in matching students to appropriate short stories. Extension of these findings to other forms of literature awaits further study.

Applications of readability knowledge are appropriate to glossing or various types of cognitive organizers, but research in such applications for literature and the interactions with reading ability have not been explored.

## Skills

Of all the content areas, English is one of the most demanding in terms of the reading skills required to understand the various genres. In addition, appreciation of the genres is a teaching goal. These requirements demand that the English teacher use every resource possible to facilitate comprehension and appreciation, including development of efficient reading skills.

In English, a convenient way of organizing reading skills seems to be around the genres. For poetry, inverted syntax, poetic vocabulary, figurative language, poetic patterns, and the use of compressed ideas require skill instruction to overcome comprehension problems (Chesler, 1976; Larocque, 1975). Reading skills demanded by drama include visualizing sets and forming action structures based on careful attention to stage instructions and dialogue. In fiction—such as the novel or short story—comprehending characters, plot, and setting; strategies for reviewing; and locating transitions are necessary reading skills. Biography demands ascertaining and evaluating the author's world view. The essay genre demands the comprehension of arguments and their organization (Larocque, 1975). Reading newspapers involves comprehension of reporting styles and application of standards of media. In addition to all the genres and media, many English classes use a grammar text which requires literal and inferential comprehension of expository text and efficient study skills. In all the above areas, there is a general demand for word attack skills and continual vocabulary development (both specialized and general).

## Strategies

Because English as a content area involves such a variety of reading demands, some writers limit themselves to discussing the reading requirements of a particular genre such as poetry, while other writers discuss strategies which they find applicable to more than one genre. However, most instructional activities fall into the three major areas of readiness, guidance in reading, and extension of understanding.

Readiness activities often seem to have two components—motivating students and overcoming initial difficulties. Often motivation is provided through self-selection of materials (Elkins, 1976; Greenlaw, 1977; Judy & Judy, 1979; Moore, 1980; Theofield, 1975). Self-selection provides the added benefit of controlling for reading difficulty if a large variety of reading levels is available in materials. Using a variety of interest inventories reading materials may be chosen and used for grouping or unit building (Lanberg, 1977). Thomas and Robinson (1977) detail activities which build suspense or interest immediately prior to reading. Detherage (1980) incorporated these activities in an English unit structured around running. Students actually ran, read about running, and wrote about running themselves. Various difficulty levels of materials were self-selected by students for assignments. Similarly, Heitzman (1979) reports that units on reading newspapers to build vocabulary and comprehension have been shown to be highly motivating for innercity children.

In addition to building motivation, overcoming initial difficulties is a concern for the English teacher. Especially for the less able reader, initial difficulty in comprehending the plot and differentiating the characters will impede attempts to finish reading. Preparing cognitive readiness may be done in several different ways: 1) advance organizers, such as overviews of characters and plot; 2) abstraction of the conflicts involved in fiction and their relationship to student experience; and 3) oral reading of the initial parts and explanatory comments or questions by the teacher (Elkins, 1976; Thomas & Robinson, 1982). Another aspect of building readiness is in the area of vocabulary. Both genre related vocabulary and general vocabulary are necessary for thorough comprehension. For example, teaching vocabulary concepts (literal and inferential) is especially important in poetry, since poetic language is often least similar to student language in its vocabulary and syntax (Chesler, 1976). A variety of techniques can be used to teach the necessary vocabulary: 1) categorical development of vocabulary through a game format (Readence & Searfoss, 1980), 2) dramatization of vocabulary through small skits (Duffelmeyer & Duffelmeyer, 1979), 3) using analogies to show relationship (Ignoffo, 1980), and 4) using modifications of the maze to teach specialized vocabulary such as metaphor, simile, rhyme, and assonance (McKenna, 1981). Additional readiness may be built by assessing and building a background in literary and social conventions necessary for students to make appropriate inferences while reading (Beach, 1980). Once the frame for reading is constructed, the teacher can set purposes for the actual reading (Elkins, 1976).

The second phase of reading instruction in English is guidance through the actual reading process. Guidance can involve the use of tapes (with or without comments) for less able readers to use as they read silently (Thomas & Robinson, 1982). Guidance can also come in the form of glosses of difficult vocabulary or syntax and the use of reading guides of various types (Dupuis & Askov, 1982; Estes & Vaughan, 1978; Singer & Donlan, 1980). Almost all types of guides focus on building different levels of comprehension such as Herber's (1978) literal, interpretive, and application guides and O'Brien and Schwarzberg's (1977) reading and reaction guides. Guides may be used individually or in small groups. For example, O'Brien and Schwarzberg provide a sample reading and reaction guide for poetry and illustrate how it could be used to direct discussion in small groups. Specialized guides such as cause-and-effect and sequence may be used to develop needed understanding (Estes & Vaughan, 1978). The guides aid students in focusing on a wider range of comprehension levels other than the literal and assist teachers in organizing their questioning at different levels (Dupuis & Askov, 1982; Styles & Cavanagh, 1980).

In addition to guides and glossing for difficult reading, some writers have taught students specific strategies for actively acquiring vocabulary and facilitating comprehension while reading. For example, students can be taught to use different types of context clues to build vocabulary (Lee, 1978). Burmeister (1976) proposed teaching older students to use the morphemic elements of English to facilitate vocabulary acquisition and overall comprehension. In the area of comprehension, various approaches have been taught. Cassidy (1978) used learning centers to teach students to apply five general reading skills to English. He attempted to facilitate transfer of skills. Readence and Moore (1979) taught secondary English students to use transactional analysis structures such as *intimacy* and *withdrawal* to analyze character relationships in short stories as they read. Crowder (1978) taught students guidelines for evaluating newspapers and magazines to facilitate their critical reading of media. The use of SQ3R would be appropriate for grammar texts, with few modifications. Analysis of connectives may be a strategy for analyzing essays.

All of the above belong to the category of metacognitive strategies students could learn and use in English class to process what they read more effectively.

The extension phase of reading involves synthesis and evaluation. Content area reading in English exhibits a growing emphasis on logical concept building through comprehension of literature and synthesizing it with other literature, concepts, and experiences. Logic is deemed a necessary condition for the appreciation of beauty. For example, one author carefully applies the logical strategies of joining and excluding in guiding students in the building of concepts and higher-order abstractions through literature (Henry, 1978). He illustrates the techniques through a poetry unit in which students develop a concept of man's relationship to nature through a process of analysis and synthesis. Related to this is the use of analogies (Bellows, 1980) in building concepts through logical relationships. Similes, metaphors, maxims, proverbs, and personification can be taught as analogies. In addition, analogies can be used to compare characters, dialogue, setting, or mood. The above extension activities are constructed on a framework of good literal and inferential comprehension but may also contribute to a process of rereading and comprehending anew.

An effective way to use the activities from the readiness, guidance, and extension phases to develop reading and thinking skills is to use or adapt the Directed Reading Activity (Dupuis & Askov, 1982; Roe, Stoodt, & Burns, 1978). As the unit plan is an efficient way to plan for developing long range reading skills in English, so the Directed Reading Activity is an efficient way to develop the reading skills necessary for a particular reading task in English, such as poetry.

White (1977) integrated many of the previously discussed suggestions in a reading development plan for the English classroom. This plan provides a broad outline for instituting and managing reading skill development using small group and large group work.

## Conclusion

What materials are available for the classroom teacher? Lists of genre-related reading skills are available (Larocque, 1975) to guide planning. For the teacher who wishes to move from single-text strategies to multitext strategies, Judy and Judy (1979) list several of the sources of junior high and senior high booklists from the National Council of Teachers of English. Columns, such as Kuykendall's "What's New in Teaching Materials?" in *The English Journal*, provides more resources. Moore (1980) provides guidelines for the use of SSR in the classroom, and Reed (1979) provides a multidimensional model for assessing the development of student attitudes toward their reading.

In light of what is being done, what needs exist in content area reading for English? As detailed before, much more research needs to be done on the instructional strategies which will be most helpful for different types of learners and most appropriate for different genres. Additionally, work on handling the reading needs of the exceptional or linguistically different in English classes should be expanded. Dupuis and Askov (1982) offer a decision-making model for meeting individual needs and discussion of some of the factors involved for the exceptional or linguistically different child. Along with Levenson (1979), they advocate adaptation of the language experience approach in the secondary school in order to meet reading needs. Since language is integral to the teaching of English and future programs may place greater demands upon the classroom teacher, additional work in these areas should be helpful. Research on the roles and relationship between the reading specialist and the English teacher could assist them in building an effective working relationship (Early, 1977; Roberts, 1978). Examination of present attitudes and practices of English teachers could provide a basis for development and implementation of content area reading programs. All these research needs are directed to assisting the classroom teacher in a demanding but rewarding task.

This overview of reading in the content area of English reveals that the development of reading skills is integral to comprehension and appreciation of literature—the goal of the English Teacher.

## Annotated Bibliography for
## Reading in English Instruction

Aulls, M., & Gelbert, F. Effects of method of instruction and ability on the literal comprehension of short stories. *Research in the teaching of English*, 1980, *14*, 51-59.
     Investigates the effects of four instructional methods on the literal comprehension of short stories by able and less able seventh grade readers. Significant results indicate vocabulary training and paced reading provided optimal results for the able reader. Paced reading was more effective for less able readers because they probably do not have to attend to the graphic code as completely during paced reading.

Beach, R. Studying the relationship between prior knowledge and response to literature. *English Journal*, 1980, *69*, 93-96.
     Asserting that knowledge of both social and literary conventions is necessary for students to make inferences, the author outlines techniques for judging students' knowledge and ascertaining how that knowledge (or lack) affects their responses to literature. Uses a technique to diagnose inferences that are difficult and then to provide knowledge or experience with other literature to build a base for inferencing.

Bellows, B.P. Running shoes are to jogging as analogies are to creative/critical thinking. *Journal of Reading*, 1980, *23*, 507-511.
     Explains the rationale behind the use of analogies to build critical/creative thinking in the content areas. Includes a basic analogies unit with applications to literature comprehension. Similes, metaphors, personification, maxims, and proverbs can be taught as analogies. Analogies can even be used in comprehension activities to compare characters, plot, setting, and mood.

Burmeister, L. Vocabulary development in content area reading through the use of morphemes. *Journal of Reading*, 1976, *19*, 481-486.

Discusses vocabulary development through study of morphemes and suggests some possible activities for the classroom.

Cassidy, J. How to read in "English." *Teacher*, 1978, *95*, 48-52.

Discusses English activities for a learning center which reinforce five reading skill areas for fourth and fifth graders. Detailed directions for making the activities are included.

Chesler, S.A. Integrating the teaching of reading and literature. *Journal of Reading*, 1976, *19*, 360-366.

Discusses the reading difficulties and skills necessary to handle the poetry genre. Sample methods are provided for choosing poems, preparing for reading, surveying, and facilitating literal and critical comprehension.

Cline, R.J.K., & Kretke, G.L. An evaluation of long term s.s.r. in the junior high school. *Journal of Reading*, 1980, *23*, 503-506.

Investigates the effects of junior high s.s.r. testing with an inventory of reading attitudes revealed that the experimental subjects had a significantly higher positive attitude toward reading than did the control subjects. S.R.A. scores showed no significant differences in reading achievement and no interaction of the treatment with intellectual capacity.

Crowder, W.W. Helping elementary students understand the news through a study of reporting styles. *Reading Improvement*, 1978, *15*, 141-144.

Describes a four step procedure to enable elementary language arts students to evaluate news reports they read and hear. Provides detailed information for the classroom teacher to build a unit based on reporting styles.

Detherage, J. Reading, writing, and running. *English Journal*, 1980, *69*, 38-41.

Building a unit around running, the author used running literature, running experiences, and personal journals after running to improve reading, writing, and communication skills. Self-selection of materials from various levels of difficulty was made. The coupling of reading, experience, and responsive writing provides a basis for verbalized concept development.

Donlan, D., & Singer, H. *Active comprehension of short stories.* Paper presented at the Annual Meeting of the Claremont Reading Conference, January 1979. (ED 170 705)

In this study on short story comprehension, the researchers investigated preposed questions and their effects on comprehension. Schema-based student-prepared questions produced significantly higher comprehension than did either teacher-prepared or general student-prepared questions. The article includes general schema questions for a short-story and illustrates how to apply them in the classroom.

Duffelmeyer, F.A., & Duffelmeyer, B.B. Developing vocabulary through dramatization. *Journal of Reading*, 1979, *23*, 141-143.

Advocates the teaching of vocabulary in language arts through dramatization of small skits. Student experience with the word in context facilitates deeper processing. Register and the use of words in various social stories can be discussed following dramatizations. The authors include a sample dramatization and how it can be used in the classroom.

Dupuis, M.M. The cloze procedure: Can it be used with literature? *Reading Improvement*, 1976, *13*, 199-203.

Dupuis, M.M. The cloze procedure as a predictor of comprehension in literature. *Journal of Educational Research*, 1980, *74*, 27-33.

    A series of studies using tenth grade students to investigate whether cloze exercises can help English teachers match student reading levels to appropriate stories. Results suggest 1) that the cloze procedure works with short stories as it does with expository writing; 2) that the scoring procedures reported, using controlled synonyms as well as exact word replacement, can make the procedure more flexible; and 3) that the cutoff scores for predicting comprehension and grouping levels may need adjustment from the 44-57 percent cutoffs reported elsewhere.

Dupuis, M.M. & Askov, E.N. *Content area reading: An individualized approach.* Englewood Cliffs, New Jersey: Prentice-Hall, 1982.

    Provides general information about diagnosing student reading skills, using a variety of grouping plans, applying a decision-making model, and organizing instruction through a unit plan. Strategies for developing vocabulary, comprehension, and study skills are included. Of special interest to the English teacher are guidelines for materials selection, ways of using language experience approach, discussions of bilingual reading, exceptional children, and dialects in the classroom. An example is given of an English concept guide for Romeo and Juliet.

Early, M. Changing content in English curriculum: Reading. In J.R. Squire (Ed.), *The teaching of English.* NSSE Yearbook, 1977, Part 1, 189-196.

    Details the positive change in attitudes toward teaching reading skills in the English classroom. Describes a variety of possible roles for English teachers in developing reading skills.

Elkins, D. *Teaching literature: Designs for cognitive development.* Columbus, Ohio: Charles E. Merrill, 1976.

    After illustrating several informal tests to evaluate students' reading abilities, the author approaches reading difficulties of students in two ways: 1) making the classroom a library with materials available for different reading levels and 2) providing preventive instruction such as text glossing, previewing, setting purposes, and reading the opening aloud.

Estes, T.H., & Vaughan, J.L., Jr. *Reading and learning in the content classroom.* Boston: Allyn & Bacon, 1978.

    After providing general information on the role of instruction and strategies for diagnosing students' reading skills, study skills, and vocabulary, the authors present a sample English unit on writing. Sample reading guides on sequence, cause-and-effect, and different comprehension levels are included along with a brief discussion of using a structured overview of concepts.

Gipe, J.P. Use of relevant context helps kids learn new word meanings. *Reading Teacher*, 1980, *33*, 398-402.

    Investigates four methods of vocabulary development (association, categories, context, and dictionary methods). The context method was significantly better for good or poor readers.

Greenlaw, M.J. *Information please.* Paper presented at the Annual Conference on Language Arts in the Elementary School, Phoenix, Arizona, April 1977 (ED 146 625)

> Proposes the term "informational books" be used in place of "nonfiction" since "informational" has no negative connotations. New informational books on selected topics are included along with a bibliography.

Guthrie, J.T. Research: Learning to criticize literature. *Journal of Reading,* 1980, *24,* 92-94.

> This internationally based study of critical literary skills under the auspices of the International Association for the Evaluation of Educational Achievement revealed students in New Zealand scored highest in comprehension. Findings indicate the New Zealand students flexibly chose different strategies to probe different stories. This critical flexibility may facilitate comprehension.

Heitzman, W.R. *The newspaper in the classroom: What research says to the teacher.* West Haven, Connecticut: National Education Association, 1979. (ED 176 284)

> This review of research on using newspapers in the classroom also includes a list of ways to use newspapers in improving reading skills, classroom discussion, and motivation in English and social studies classrooms. A list of resources along with guidelines for beginning such a program are included.
>
> Use of the newspaper is shown to be highly motivating to innercity children, according to several studies and programs. Several activities concerned with vocabulary and main ideas are included.

Henry, G.H. *Teaching reading as concept development: Emphasis on affective thinking.* Newark, Delaware: International Reading Association, 1978.

> Attempting to close the gap between literature teachers and reading teachers, the author proposes that reading for concept development involves thinking through written language to discover relations and to structure them tentatively. Synthesis of relations is concept development. Developing the acts of joining, excluding, selecting, and implying through study of literature examples, the author illustrates how logical strategies can help students structure concepts through reading and relate them to other experiences, other concepts, and other reading. A sample unit in literature is included.

Herber, H.L. *Teaching reading in the content areas* (2nd ed.). Englewood Cliffs, New Jersey: Prentice-Hall, 1978.

> Develops a philosophy of content area reading and proposes a three level guide to aid comprehension (literal, interpretive, and application). The author emphasizes patterns and relationships which he illustrates in different content areas.

Ignoffo, M.F. The thread of thought: Analogies as a vocabulary building method. *Journal of Reading,* 1980, *23,* 519-521.

> Viewing analogies as an abbreviated form of sentence completion in which the reader supplies part of the context, the author provides examples of classroom use of analogies to build English vocabulary. Additionally, the author lists and illustrates different logical structures of analogies.

Judy, S.N., & Judy, S.J. *The English teacher's handbook.* Cambridge, Massachusetts: Winthrop, 1979.

> Full of activities and possible resources in reading for the English teacher, this text emphasizes individualization and variety in the chapter on reading. Reading skills (general or genre-related), diagnosis, grouping, and design of units are not detailed.

LaRocque, G.E. Developing special skills for reading genres. *Reading Improvement*, 1977, *14*, 182-186.

LaRocque, G.E. *We weren't born literate: Reading the "genres."* Paper presented at the Plains Regional Conference of the International Reading Association, St. Louis, February 1975. (ED 103 833)
    Discusses in detail some of the comprehension problems for different literary genres such as poetry, drama, short stories, essays, novels, and biographies. Ways of enabling students to surmount some of the difficulties of form are discussed.

Lanberg, W.J. Helping reluctant readers help themselves: Interest inventories. *English Journal*, 1977, *66*, 40-44.
    Several types of interest inventories are presented along with a description of how they can be used to increase student reading in and outside English class.

Lee, J. Increasing comprehension through use of context clue categories. *Journal of Reading*, 1978, *22*, 259-261.
    The author details the use of seven types of context clues a teacher may use to increase comprehension. A teacher may develop exercises teaching the use of one particular type of clue using content materials. Material with deletions can be presented and students can pose possible substitutions. One type of word such as nouns or verbs may be deleted to assess how students use syntactic clues of English.

Levenson, S. Teaching reading and writing to limited and non-English speakers in secondary schools. *English Journal*, 1979, *68*, 38-42.
    Describes the rationale for using language experience for persons who are transitional English speakers. Using art, experience, and discussion, the teacher can give them opportunities to produce highly meaningful reading material which uses known vocabulary.

Lucking, R.A. A study of the effects of hierarchically-ordered questioning techniques on adolescents' responses to short stories. *Research in the Teaching of English*, 1976, *10*, 269-276.
    Investigates the effects of hierarchically-ordered comprehension questions based on the Bloom-Clegg taxonomy. Students read short stories and wrote essays which were analyzed as a repeated measure. Findings indicate significantly more interpretation by students after the use of hierarchically-ordered questions. In addition, students exhibited a more positive attitude after this treatment.

McKenna, M.C. A modified maze approach to teaching poetry. *Journal of Reading*, 1981, *24*, 391-394.
    After describing the maze procedure, the author illustrates how the maze technique can be used to teach metrics, assonance, onomatopoeia, metaphor, simile, personification, rhyme, sensory appeal, and diction.

Moore, J.C. Guidelines for secondary s.s.r. Washington, D.C.: Department of Health, Education, and Welfare, 1980 (ED 195 955)
    Provides guidelines for using s.s.r. in the secondary classroom effectively. A list of possible materials for reading and discussion in the English classroom is included along with other content areas.

O'Brien, D., & Schwarzberg, S. A strategy for improving teenagers' understanding and appreciation of poetry. *Journal of Reading*, 1977, *30*, 381-386.
> Proposes using reading and reaction guides for poetry with small groups in secondary English. A sample guide for a poem and directions for classroom use are included.

Pressley, M., Levin, J.R., & Miller, G.E. How does the keyword method affect vocabulary, comprehension and usage? *Reading Research Quarterly*, 1981, *16*, 213-226.
> Reports the results of four related studies. The experimental group was taught a strategy of taking the familiar part of a new word, such as *cat* from *catkin*, and forming an image merging the familiar meaning with the obscure meaning. Findings indicated significant differences between control subjects and experimental subjects when subjects were tested in a variety of ways in the four studies.

Purves, A.C., & Rippere, V. *Elements of writing about a literary work: A study of response to literature.* Champaign, Illinois: National Council of Teachers of English, 1968.

Readence, J.E., & Moore, D. Responding to literature: An alternative to questioning. *Journal of Reading*, 1979, *23*, 107-111.
> Proposes an alternative to study guide questions for junior and senior high school English teachers. Believing that study guides only indirectly teach comprehension strategies, the authors attempted to provide students with structures to evaluate literature concepts while reading. The authors used Harris' six transactional analysis structures to examine character relationships. After defining each structure (such as intimacy or withdrawal) and giving an example of its application to a poem, the authors propose a procedure for teaching students how to use these structures to process literature meaningfully as they read.

Readence, J.E., & Searfoss, L.W. Teaching strategies for vocabulary development. *English Journal*, 1980, *69*, 43-46.
> Includes several general games for the English classroom to facilitate categorical development of vocabulary words. The categorization of vocabulary can be applied to comprehension of literature by guiding ways of thinking about characters.

Readence, J.E., & Searfoss, L.W. *Reading in the content area of language arts.* Montgomery: Alabama State Department of Education, 1975. (ED 189 572)
> Illustrates how reading instruction can be combined with other aspects of language arts. Vocabulary, comprehension, and study skills are presented with sample activities in this handbook for the language arts teacher.

Reed, K. Assessing affective responses to reading: A multidimensional model. *Reading World*, 1979, *19*, 149-156.
> Discusses advantages and disadvantages of a variety of reactive and nonreactive methods of measuring. Outlines a multi-measurement model of assessment of student attitudes toward reading.

Roberts, D.E. The two-ended candle: Reading and English. *English Journal*, 1978, *67*, 54-56.
> Discusses briefly fundamental questions about the relationship between the English teacher and secondary reading instruction. The author states that English teachers can and should work with reading teachers to develop reading skills.

Robinson, H.A. *Teaching reading and study strategies: The content areas* (2nd ed.). Boston: Allyn & Bacon, 1978.

Discusses the specific strategies students must develop in order to comprehend the various genres such as the short story and drama. The author proposes a traditional analysis framework for discussion (exposition and argument/narration and description). The analysis of literature using a Profundity Scale may be of interest to the classroom teacher as a way to direct analysis at different comprehension levels. Included are a sample of adapting materials and a sample concept guide.

Roe, B.D., Stoodt, B.D., & Burns, P.C. *Reading instruction in secondary schools.* Chicago: Rand McNally, 1978.

After providing general comprehension and vocabulary building information for the content areas, the authors provide a section for the language arts teacher. Aiding students in understanding vocabulary such as *haiku* or *adjective* and the design of various literature genres is first developed. The comprehension instructional strategy creating a framework of reading readiness, establishing purposes, reading, discussion, and extension. A sample literature lesson is included.

Singer, H., & Donlan, D. *Reading and learning from text.* Boston: Little, Brown, 1980.

Uses a topical unit in English literature to illustrate single text strategies (gloss, DRA, learning-from-text guides, and SQ3R) and multitext strategies (concept development, inquiry, and projects). Does not include specific guidance in vocabulary development.

Soltis, J.M., & Pflaum, S.W. The effect of instruction in connectives on reading comprehension. *Reading World*, 1979, *19*, 179-184.

Investigates the effects of instruction in connectives on the comprehension of seventh and eighth grade innercity ethnic subjects. A significant effect of instruction was found on a cloze-like Connective Test but not on the Standard Test Lessons in Reading.

Styles, K., & Cavanagh, G. Language across the curriculum: The art of questioning and responding. *English Journal*, 1980, *69*, 24-27.

Argues for developing student thinking through abstract representation of thoughts and feelings in precise language. Believing that different types of thinking skills are fostered by different questioning levels, the authors discuss using a school language policy to enable students to grasp logical thinking patterns by responding to questioning at different levels.

Theofield, M.B. ESSO *self-concept and basic reading in a secondary school program.* Paper presented at the annual Convention of the International Reading Association, New York City, May 1975. (ED 110 951)

A description of an integrated English-social studies curriculum for secondary students with learning problems, this article details the integration of reading and study skills, coping skills, special education, and the building of self-concept in the English and social studies content areas. Grouping was based on skill needs. The personal journal was a key part of the English curriculum as a basis for composition correction, language experience (reading it aloud), and private communication with the teacher. Contracting for reading skills and assignments was also used in the English classroom.

Thomas, E.L., & Robinson, H.A. *Improving reading in every class* (3rd ed.). Boston: Allyn & Bacon, 1982.

In addition to general strategies for building comprehension and vocabulary, the authors have presented specific activities which the English teacher may use to build readiness, provide advance organizers and overcome initial reading difficulties. A sample reading guide for comprehension and vocabulary building games and activities is included.

Weisberg, R.A. A comparison of good and poor readers' ability to comprehend explicit and implicit information in short stories based on two modes of presentation. *Research in the Teaching of English*, 1979, *13*, 337-351.

Investigates fourth grade readers' comprehension of six short stories presented through visual and auditory modes and tested through free and probed recall. Three types of inferencing were probed. Differences between good and poor readers in memory for basic idea units in both free recall and probed recall, regardless of mode of presentation, supports a general language comprehension deficit in poor readers.

White, R.H. Reading skills in the English class. *Clearing House*, 1977, *51*, 32-35.

Outlines a plan of integrating and managing the development of reading skills in English. Suggests a program of free reading, interest-centered projects, teacher-directed units, and planned development of language skills. Contains several charts to facilitate planning and management of small and large group work.

# Reading in the
# Content Area of Foreign Language

John E. Carlson
*Williamsport, Pennsylvania, Area High School*

## Overview

In the classroom the foreign language teacher must deal with reading skill in a manner similar to the elementary teacher at the primary level, to the reading teacher improving skills at any level, and to the English teacher emphasizing content at the secondary and college levels. Acquiring reading skill in a second language involves the student in using techniques and strategies which were used in learning the mother tongue. In order to be successful in teaching students to read in a second language, the teacher must realize the enormity and complexity of this task.

The purpose of this overview is to help foreign language educators recognize this fact and guide them to further sources of information. The accompanying annotated bibliography offers a collection of books and articles published between 1975 and 1981, providing examples and details of the major points here.

Just as children learn their first language, reading in a second language is part of a natural sequence of language acquisition. Before children read or learn to read, they are exposed to oral/aural experiences. Passive understanding of sounds, however, does not guarantee acquisition of the reading skill.

The foreign language teacher should provide the same opportunities for learning to read which elementary and reading teachers do:

> In teaching reading in a foreign language, aims, procedures, and techniques can be virtually the same as those once used for the acquisition of the reading skill in the mother tongue. (de Oliveira, 1978, p. 187)

Vocabulary, learning, context clues, exercises, activities, drills, reading strategies, and techniques all should be incorporated into the foreign language curriculum (Mackay et al., 1979; Madsen & Bowen, 1978; Papalia, 1976).

Transition from the process of learning to read in a second language to reading to learn is a major step and indicates the crossover into content reading. Given the limited exposure to a foreign tongue in the United States, even advanced language students have difficulty with this transition, which represents one of the major problems in foreign language pedagogy.

## Skills

Teachers supply materials and use texts with cultural information concerning the countries where the language is spoken or literary selections from prominent authors in those countries, and the learner often gives up in frustration, since the readings are well beyond the student's comprehension level (Schulz, 1981). In order to ascertain the reading level and diagnose the competency of students, cloze procedures have been adapted for implementation in several of the foreign languages (Briere et al., 1978). This tool can also be used as a vocabulary learning device in the classroom. To match reading materials, textbook passages, and literature with the reading level of students, formulas and graphs have also been formulated for languages other than English. They include: the FRASE graph, and the Spaulding, Lix, and Flesch formulas (Vari-Cartier, 1981). Specific materials for evaluating textbooks in foreign languages are available (Madsen & Bowen, 1978).

Content readings can serve students in cultural analysis of language and ideas if they are at their instructional or independent reading level. However, if they fall within the frustration level of reading they become useless and even destructive of the learner's motivation to continue study of the language. Indeed, as Anastos (1981, p. 128) maintains, "Reading and understanding a literary text in the foreign language is a challenging objective for students." Often the sequence of courses at the secondary and college levels takes students from graded readers with a limited high frequency vocabulary directly into the reading of literature which surveys the great works and authors in that language. Without prereading exercises and instruction students are faced with an overwhelming task and yet they realize the importance of acquiring the reading skill since the majority of advanced courses are literature courses, and doctoral candidates must often pass examinations in foreign language reading comprehension (Davison, 1976; Kinsella, 1978; Phillips, 1978).

To become fluent in content reading, students need to read for global meaning rather than translating or word by word plodding through a page or passage. It is not reading if students stop several times on each line to check English equivalents. Of course, recurring new words should be checked in a dictionary after reading a section the first time or perhaps preceding a second reading of the passage. Strategies and skills used in the decoding process in the mother tongue must not be ignored while learning the second language. Common sense indicates that English dictionaries are not banned for usage when students read in English. Realia such as signs, announcements, and posters also should be prevalent in the foreign language classroom (Cziko, 1978; Greenewald, 1981; Kinsella, 1978, Phillips, 1978). Specific reading skill activities can be used with good results; a variety are available (Mackay et al., 1979; Papalia, 1976; Piercey, 1982).

Besides teaching the reading skill, foreign language teachers must also teach the skills and rules of oral understanding, speaking, writing, syntax, and grammar (Binkley, 1978; Cziko, 1978). These facets of language learning combine to create an enormous and complex task for both the student and the teacher. At least with the help of the information collected in the following bibliography, foreign language teachers will be better equipped to teach the important skill of reading. Assuredly, learners will experience satisfaction when they arrive successfully at that crucial moment of being able to read and comprehend unfamiliar material containing new information and ideas (i.e., content reading in the foreign language).

## Annotated Bibliography for
## Reading in Foreign Language Instruction

Anastos, Perry. Probing a short story with language exercises. *Foreign Language Annals*, 1981, *14*, 127-132.
    The challenge of reading a short story or any other literary piece in the foreign language with comprehension hinges substantially on prior knowledge of the vocabulary to be encountered. In order to prepare the student for a reading, several vocabulary drills can be constructed. Examples of reading enrichment exercises are presented in this article including substitution, completion, and paraphrasing. The entire reading unit is discussed with emphasis on vocabulary comprehension in context. Preceding a teacher-student discussion of the content of the short story, both written question and answer exercises and an oral summary delivered by the teacher are incorporated into this unit designed for an advanced high school class.

Binkley, Janet R. Oral reading can be an FL motivator. *Foreign Language Annals*, 1978, *11*, 289-290.

Adapted from the format of an annual contest in West Germany, the oral reading activity in the foreign language classroom draws on the students' ability to read aloud effectively, to convey the joy of literature. Participants select a passage from a content or literary book in the foreign language and read to their classmates. This procedure involves phrasing, intonation, pronunciation, accent, vocabulary expansion, and listening comprehension.

Benseler, David P. (Ed.). ACTFL *annual bibliography of books and articles on pedagogy in foreign languages for the years 1977 and 1978*. American Council on the Teaching of Foreign Languages, 1980.

This bibliography represents the tenth such compilation edited by ACTFL and includes more than 150 journals and reference sources. Divided into specific topics and areas, this work is most valuable for educators concerned with reading in the foreign language classroom. Relevant headings include: Linguistics, Vocabulary and Language Development, Teaching Foreign Literature, Developmental and Cultural Reading Materials, Physiology and Psychology of Language Learning, Curriculum, Methods, and Skills Learning.

Bloom, K.E., & Shuell, T.J. Effects of massed and distributed practice on the learning and retention of second language vocabulary. *Journal of Educational Research*, 1981, *74*, 245-248.

This study suggests that vocabulary learning is improved when foreign students practice new words in small time periods on consecutive days rather than one massed drill. A variety of vocabulary exercises is also presented. The implications of the findings for classroom instruction and the need to distinguish between learning and memory are discussed.

Briere, E.J., Clausing, G., Senko, D., & Purcell, E. A look at cloze testing across language and levels. *Modern Language Journal*, 1978, *62*, 23-26.

Despite procedural problems and limitations the cloze activity can be used to signify achievement levels of language students in German, Japanese, Russian, and Spanish. Japanese needs to be transcribed using the Latin alphabet. The Cyrillic alphabet of Russian affects results, and all four languages present syntactical problems. Nevertheless, the cloze procedure affords the foreign language educator with a tool for diagnostic and placement purposes.

Cziko, Gary. Differences in first and second language reading: The use of syntactic, semantic, and discourse constraints. *Canadian Modern Language Review*, 1978, *34*, 473-489.

If learners use syntactic, semantic, and discourse clues when reading in the mother tongue it is not necessarily assumable that they will employ these same means in reading in the foreign language. The teacher must point out and provide the opportunity to practice the aids to reading provided by word order, grammar rules, meaning, and general topic.

Davison, W.F. Factors in evaluating and selecting texts for the foreign language classroom. *English Language Teaching Journal*, 1976, *30*, 310-314.

Author stresses the importance of matching the textbook in the foreign language classroom with the needs and objectives of the students. The content of readings should be in the appropriate register whether formal, conversational, or literary. The selection of a text involves asking the question: What skills will be needed by the student?

de Oliveira, S.R. Transition from an aural/oral stage to the teaching of reading in a foreign language. *English Language Teaching Journal*, 1978, *32*, 181-187.

    Maintains that the procedures and teaching techniques used for the acquisition of reading skills for the mother tongue are applicable for foreign language learning. Learners should begin reading passages which already have been introduced and practiced orally. Reading exercises should be varied and numerous, including written work which serves as a reinforcer.

Greenewald, M.J. Developing and using cloze materials to teach reading. *Foreign Language Annals*, 1981, *14*, 185-188.

    Author reveals how the cloze procedure can be used as an instructional device rather than as a diagnostic instrument or test. The standard format and administration of a cloze exercise can be followed with an ensuing class review. Study of acceptable answers and synonyms might be incorporated. Modifications of the tool can also be made such as multiple-choice selections, word-length clues, and exact number of letters. Another objective in employing cloze as an instructional exercise is to teach mature reading strategies in comparison to word-by-word reading.

Grittner, F.M. *Teaching foreign languages* (2nd ed.). New York: Harper & Row, 1977.

    This methodology textbook is intended for the teacher of foreign languages in the elementary school and at the secondary and undergraduate levels. It contains a systematic and objective presentation of various successful methods of teaching foreign languages in American schools, both past and present. Step-by-step procedures for teaching reading at the primer, intermediate, and liberated (advanced) stages of language acquisition are presented along with examples. Topics such as learning vocabulary in context, the skill of reading, and achievement testing in oral and silent reading ability are discussed. Included is a suggested curriculum in French, German, and Spanish for levels I through IV with minimal attainment levels of reading skills and content.

Kinsella, V. *Language teaching and linguistics: Surveys.* Cambridge: Cambridge University Press, 1978.

    This collection of articles includes surveys of recent research and theories in the fields of applied linguistics and foreign language teaching. The authors discuss advanced reading skills, the teaching of English as a foreign language, preliminary classroom activities to reading, intensive reading, and extensive reading. A bibliography of related articles and books by authors from many countries follows each survey. This work is intended as both an overview for language teachers and a guide for language specialists.

Lange, D.L., & Clausing, G. An examination of two methods of generating and scoring cloze tests with students of German on three levels. *Modern Language Journal*, 1981, *65*, 254-261.

    Included within this article is a review of the construction and scoring of a cloze test in German. Rather than an instrument for level of reading difficulty, the German cloze test is employed as a proficiency test for purposes such as course placement. Two methods of construction are presented: the usual Nth format omitting every fifth word and a random format wherein the administrator decides which words are to be deleted. Also, two ways of scoring are examined: the exact word versus acceptable answer. Following an actual cloze test administration the results are discussed in reference to the reliability of the findings.

Mackay, R., Barkman, B., & Jordan, B.R. (Eds.). *Reading in a second language: Hypotheses, organization, and practice.* Rowley, Massachusetts: Newbury House, 1979.

Discusses theories of the reading process (hypotheses), comprehension and interpretation skills (organization), and skill-building activities (practice).

Madsen, H.S., & Bowen, J.D. *Adaptation in language teaching.* Rowley, Massachusetts: Newbury House, 1978.

A general methodology text for foreign language teachers. Good sections on text evaluation and adapting materials.

Papalia, A. *Learner centered language teaching, methods, and materials.* Rowley, Massachusetts: Newbury House, 1976.

A general methodology text for foreign language teachers. Chapters on culture, listening, speaking, and grammar instruction, as well as reading comprehension. Section evaluating foreign language textbooks.

Phillips, J.K. Reading is communication, too! *Foreign Language Annals*, 1978, *11*, 281-287.

By surrounding the student with written messages found in the foreign country, emphasis is on the ability to interpret culturally authentic messages. The learner will become functionally literate in the second language. Traditional classroom reading materials have been artificial in contrast to real-life messages. This article identifies communicative realia, strategies for decoding, and evaluative techniques. The objective of reaching the independent level of reading is dependent on the increasing language skills of the learner linked with contextual expectations involving guessing and prediction.

Piercey, D. *Reading activities in content areas: An ideabook for middle and secondary schools* (2nd ed.). Boston: Allyn & Bacon, 1982.

Suggests reading activities and teaching strategies to encourage students' success in several content areas including foreign languages. Focuses on classroom techniques for stimulating vocabulary development and generating understanding and details activities for practicing the skills necessary for learning success in each area. Suggested level, objectives, required student and teacher preparation, and specific procedures are outlined for each activity (Chapter 7, pp. 183-198).

Schulz, R.A. Literature and readability: Bridging the gap in foreign language reading. *Modern Language Journal*, 1981, *65*, 43-53.

Foreign language learners need to comprehend reading selections and materials with minimal levels of frustration. The sequence of texts and literary works presented to the student must recognize this need; otherwise, the reading activity becomes useless and often destructive in terms of the learner's attitude toward reading in the foreign language. This article stresses the importance of measuring the readability level of selections by applying objective analytical instruments coupled with the subjective judgment of the language instructor. The fault of many language programs has been a gap between the usage of structured graded readers and textbooks containing a high-frequency, limited vocabulary at the beginning and intermediate levels to a literary survey course of master works at the advanced level of foreign language curriculum.

Swaffer, J.K., & Woodruff, M.S. Language for comprehension: Focus on reading—a report on the University of Texas German program. *Modern Language Journal*, 1978, *62*, 27-32.

A pilot program at the University of Texas at Austin introduces reading for global meaning in the fifth week of beginning language instruction. After four weeks of oral interaction with the students involving teacher directives and commands, students begin reading for main idea comprehension. The underlying hypothesis is that second language learning is more efficient and successful when the more difficult, productive language skills of speaking and writing follow understanding and reading. It was found that students attitudes improved toward foreign language study with the implementation of this program. Above average percentile scores in the Modern Language Association standardized listening and reading tests were also noted.

Vari-Cartier, P. Development and validation of a new instrument to assess the readability of Spanish prose. *Modern Language Journal*, 1981, *65*, 141-148.

In contrast to the Spaulding method for measuring readability of Spanish prose the FRASE instrument presented here is easy and convenient. First developed in 1956 the Spaulding formula is based on word frequencies and complex calculations which are often beyond the capabilities and time demands of the classroom teacher. The new FRASE (Fry Readability Adaptation for Spanish Evaluation) technique counts the number of sentences and syllables per 100 words and using an adapted Fry Graph determines the reading difficulty of the passage according to Spanish I, II, III or IV rather than the Fry grade level designation.

# Reading in the
# Content Area of Mathematics

James F. Nolan
*Lafayette College*

## Overview

This report which summarizes a review of current literature (1957-1981) on the topic of reading in the content area of mathematics is divided into several sections: a review of the difficulties which are inherent in reading math, a review of empirical research concerning the reading of math, a description of essential skills, a discussion of possible strategies for promoting skill development, and a discussion of procedures for assessing the readability of math materials.

Reading specialists and mathematics teachers generally agree that there are several factors which make the reading of math materials inherently difficult. In general, math texts are written in a terse, unimaginative style, offer few verbal context clues to help in decoding meaning, and lack the redundancy which one finds in most writing (Hollander, 1977; Manzo, 1975; Munro, 1979; Wesley & Tanner, 1980). Math also tends to be highly compact and requires very slow, deliberate reading in order to comprehend the concepts (Bye, 1975; Krulik, 1980). Adding to the math student's problems is the fact that mathematical symbols (e.g., =) do not express the typical phoneme-grapheme relationship and, thus, they must be memorized (Dunlap & McKnight, 1978). An additional complicating factor is the variety of eye movements which are required to read math in addition to the normal left to right movements (Georgia State Department of Education, 1975). Examples of the various eye movements required are:

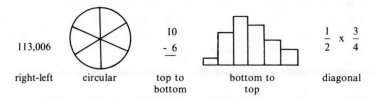

| right-left | circular | top to bottom | bottom to top | diagonal |

In addition to the general problems which are outlined above, math presents specific reading problems in the areas of vocabulary or concept development and word problems. O'Mara (1981) has identified five different contexts in which math concepts may be presented: pictorial or graphic, symbolic or computational, verbal, textual, and testing. These five different contexts may be used to present four different types of vocabulary: words which have the same meaning as they do in general usage, technical words which are peculiar to math (polynomial), symbolic vocabulary (M), and words which have multiple meanings (Riley & Pachtman, 1978). Words with multiple meanings are those words which have meaning in general usage and a different meaning in math (root, property), and also words which have general meanings and two technical meanings (base, square). This list of specific difficulties in learning math vocabulary clearly points out the need for skill instruction in that area.

Word problems also contain many pitfalls for the prospective student of mathematics who has not previously developed the necessary reading skills. An inability to solve word problems successfully often becomes a major stumbling block to success in math. Singer and Donlan (1980) cite several potential problems, including the use of synonyms rather than words actually used in formulas, e.g., rate instead of speed; the presentation of information in the problem in an order which is different from that used in the formula; and the presentation of insufficient or extraneous information.

## Review of Empirical Research

Empirical research concerning the reading of mathematics has concentrated in three major areas: word problem solving, vocabulary development, and general factors related to the ability to read math.

As early as 1970, Earp reported the existence of a fairly large body of research which indicated that specific instruction in reading of math word problems leads to improved problem solving by pupils.

Rewriting word problems to make them easier to read and to pattern them after the oral language of students seems to be an effective strategy for facilitating problem solving (Cohen & Stover, 1981; McCabe, 1977). Cohen and Stover also identified the variables which are important factors to keep in mind when one is rewriting word problems to make them easier: simplifying vocabulary, reducing sentence length, adding diagrams, changing the order in which the information is presented to mimic the use of information in the formula, and removing extraneous information. Rubens (1980) studied the problem solving abilities of two groups of students. One group was instructed by a math teacher who had little background in reading and thus concentrated on math skills. The other group was instructed by a reading teacher who had little math background and thus concentrated on teaching reading skills. Those students who were instructed by the reading teacher were able to solve math word problems more efficiently.

Research concerning the effects of providing specific skill instruction in the area of math vocabulary has added support to the importance of teaching reading skills in math classes. Using gain scores on the Stanford Diagnostic tests in math vocabulary and problem solving as the dependent variables, Skrypa (1979) found that teaching math vocabulary led to improved scores in both vocabulary and problem solving. Kruse (1979) also found that teaching math vocabulary is an effective strategy irrespective of the particular teaching approach used.

There has been research of a more general nature, as well. O'Mara (1981) estimated that approximately 35 percent of the errors on math achievement tests may actually be due to problems in reading. She also found that there is a difference between reading ability and problem solving ability but that good problem solvers seem to have a significantly greater knowledge of math vocabulary than poor problem solvers. Elliot and Wiles (1979) gave cloze procedures developed from an eighth grade math text to 91 math teachers in a large urban school system. Five percent of the teachers scored at the frustration level and 22 percent scored at the instructional level. Finally, Bye (1975) attempted to link reading problems in math to a lack of cognitive development as defined by Piaget. She found that 80 percent of the tenth graders and 65 percent of the twelfth graders were unable to keep track of four attributes—size, color, shape, texture—at one time.

There is great need for future experimental research in the area of reading in mathematics but, at present, researchers have shown several strong links between reading skills, knowledge of math vocabulary, and problem solving ability.

# Skills

The specific skills which are required to read math may be separated into five general areas: 1) perceiving and decoding symbols; 2) attaching literal meaning or concept development; 3) interpreting literal meanings in terms of mathematical symbols or inferential comprehension; 4) applying these interpretations to the solution of word problems; and 5) using specialized study skills (Ciani, 1981; Earle, 1976; Pachtman & Riley, 1978).

Specific skills required to perceive and decode symbols are the ability to associate words with proper symbols; the ability to express ideas in objects and pictures; and the awareness that symbols have more than one meaning, e.g.—as in $\overline{AB}$, $1/2$, $\div$ (Florida State Department of Education, 1975) as well as the ability to recognize words on sight (Ciani, 1981; Earle, 1976).

Specific skills required for concept or vocabulary development are: attaching precise definitions to mathematical concepts (Florida, 1975); using verbal, graphic, and symbolic context clues (Ciani, 1981; Earle, 1976; Florida, 1975); using roots, prefixes, and suffixes as a means of structural analysis (Ciani, 1981; Earle, 1976); and interpreting words with special or multiple meanings (Florida, 1975; Georgia, 1975).

Specific skills required for interpreting the literal meanings in symbols include understanding the main idea (Dunlap & McKnight, 1978); understanding supporting details (Hollander, 1977); interpreting graphs and recognizing the reversability of math sentences, e.g., $4 = 1 + 3$ (Florida, 1975); interpreting formulas and equations (Henrichs & Sisson, 1980); and interpreting specialized mathematical notation (Morrison, 1980).

Specific skills required for solving word problems include analyzing the given information and identifying it as sufficient, insufficient, or extraneous (Florida, 1975); using the appropriate sequence clues (Henrich & Sisson, 1980); translating from general language to mathematical terms to numerical symbols and back again to general meaning (Dunlap & McKnight, 1978); and understanding the facts of the problem, the mathematical concepts implied, and the numerical depiction of the problem (Pachtman & Riley, 1978).

Specialized study skills which are required for math include adjusting one's reading rate (Earle, 1976; Florida, 1975; Henrich & Sisson, 1980); reading with paper and pencil (Florida, 1975); using parts of the book to develop locational skills (Earle, 1976; Henrich & Sisson, 1980); following directions (Hollander, 1977); using mathematicl dictionaries (Alabama, 1975; Ciani, 1981; Earle, 1976); using special study formulas, doing voluntary readings in math (Florida, 1975); and employing appropriate test taking strategies (Morrison, 1980).

## Strategies

This section of the paper discusses strategies which have been recommended to promote development of the reading skills which were discussed in the previous section. General strategies for enhancing mathematical reading will be discussed first, followed by strategies for promoting development of specific skills.

General strategies which are especially helpful in developing the ability to read mathematics successfully are similar to the strategies which are used in other content areas. These include the use of directed reading activities, marginal glosses, study and reading guides, the use of multiple texts, and units of instruction which incorporate reading activities into daily math classes (Dupuis & Askov, 1982; Herber, 1978; Shepherd, 1982; Singer & Donlan, 1980; Thomas & Robinson, 1977). Allowing students to manipulate concrete objects physically, using kinesthetic and visual aids to provide additional clues, and providing opportunities to practice oral expression of concepts before encountering them in reading are additional general strategies which seem to be effective in developing reading skills for math (Aiken, 1977; Hollander, 1977).

To aid students in the skill area of recognizing and decoding symbols, suggested activities are to provide practice in matching words, symbols, and math expressions, e.g. = EQUALS 8 ? 4 x 2 (Krulik, 1980); to have students practice writing the math symbols for words and expressions which are read orally by the teacher (Florida, 1975); to use flash cards which contain words, symbols, and math expressions (Alabama, 1976); to use puzzles and word find exercises which require students to circle key words (Ciani, 1981); and to provide practice in oral pronunciation of words, symbols, and expressions (Hollander, 1977). The teacher may facilitate student recognition of the proper direction in which to read math symbols by having students draw arrows to indicate the proper order of oral expression (Georgia, 1975).

Several strategies which are effective in promoting vocabulary or concept development were also identified in the review of the literature. The use of structured overviews and advance organizers which depict graphically the relationship between new concept words and those concepts which were previously learned is highly recommended (Dupuis & Askov, 1982; Riley & Pachtman, 1978; Thelen, 1979).

Matching exercises, multiple choice exercises, and crossword puzzles may be used to help refine students' understanding of key concepts (Florida, 1975). Providing practice in the use of context clues is an excellent strategy for promoting vocabulary development. One suggested strategy is to provide a clue in math symbols which the student uses to decode a verbal sentence, e.g., "$10 \div 5 = 2$, we call five a *divisor*" (Florida, 1975). This technique is actually a refinement of the modified cloze procedure. The cloze procedure may also be used to promote and test for concept development. Practice in using word attack skills, such as the use of roots, prefixes, and suffixes, is also helpful in enhancing vocabulary development. Multi-syllabic words such as equilateral and equiangular may be broken into component parts and decoded more easily (Earle, 1976; Florida, 1975). One final suggestion for promoting vocabulary development is to require students to maintain a notebook ("dictionary") of technical math terms (polynomial) and general terms (base) which are used in a special way in math (Krulik, 1980).

Suggestions for strategies to promote skills which are important for interpreting literal meanings are not as plentiful as they are in other skill areas. The Florida report suggests that teachers routinely question students regarding the main ideas of reading passages and the supporting details which develop the main idea. To help students learn how to interpret graphs, the same report (1975) suggests that teachers give students a graph in which the axes are not labeled and require the students to label the graph in response to specific interpretations made by the teacher. Finally, Henrichs and Sisson (1980) suggest that students be given specific practice in reading and interpreting formulas and equations orally.

Strategies to help students develop problem solving abilities, on ⟵ the other hand, are abundant. One effective strategy is for the teacher to rewrite the problems or to have brighter students rewrite the word problems by patterning them after their own oral language (Cohen & Stover, 1981; McCabe, 1977; Wesley & Tanner, 1980). Teaching specific vocabulary and concept terms as they apply to word problems is another effective strategy (Kruse, 1979; Rubens, 1980). Godfrey (1979) suggests the use of review lessons in which word problems are used to review key concepts as an effective strategy for promoting both vocabulary development and problem solving. Teaching students to use the proper sequence of steps in solving word problems may be facilitated by cutting up word problems (from old books) into separate sentences, scrambling the order and then requiring the students to reassemble the problems in the proper sequence (Florida, 1975). The Florida report also suggests that teachers must provide practice in indentifying sufficient, insufficient, and extraneous information.

Study guides may also be helpful in teaching students how to attack word problems. Riley and Pachtman (1978) suggest using a three-level study guide for word problems. Level one deals with the facts of the problem; level two deals with the math concepts; and level three deals with the numerical symbols used in solving the problem. For all three levels they suggest using multiple choice items in the study guide. Dunlap and McKnight (1978) also advocate the use of reading guides for teaching word problem solving, but they point out that students must be moved gradually from dependence on the study guide to independence in problem solving.

Several specialized procedures or formulas for attacking word problems have also been developed to aid teachers in teaching skills necessary for problem solving. Manzo (1975) developed the ReQuest procedure for problem solving. In using this procedure, teacher and students read each sentence of the word problem, and after each sentence, they ask each other questions to clarify the concepts involved in the problem. This procedure continues until the entire problem has been read and discussed. Earle (1976) suggests the following formula for attacking word problems: read the entire problem quickly, read it again and state the given information, change the general terms to mathematical symbols, do the computation, label the answer, decide if the answer seems sensible, recheck the computation, change the answer back to general terms. A final formula for solving word problems has been offered by Singer and Donaln (1980). Their formula is the $RQ_4S_2T$ formula: $R$ead the problem, Q1–What facts are given?, Q2—What do I have to find out?, Q3—What shall I let X equal?, Q4—How shall I represent the other information?, S1—Set up the equation, S2—Solve the equation, $T$est the answer.

The Florida report suggests several strategies for developing the specialized study skills which are important in math. Among these strategies are: providing practice in scanning and summarizing as well as reading slowly and deliberately; assigning students to compute example problems as they are reading to develop the habit of reading with paper and pencil; using scavenger hunts to practice using the parts of the book and develop locational skills. Devine (1979) points out the importance of paying special attention to the structure of the book, and Robinson (1975) suggests the following procedure for students to follow in reading math books: (re)read the verbal definitions; read the explanatory information, both symbolic and graphic; reread the explanatory information; and reread the verbal definition if necessary. Other specialized study formulas which may be useful for reading math are SQ3R—survey, question, read, recite, review (Singer & Donlan, 1980); and PQ4R—preview, question, read, reflect, recite, review (Maffei, 1973; Thomas & Robinson, 1977).

## Materials

This section on materials will deal with specialized procedures for assessing the readability of math materials and matching texts to students.

The most appropriate measure of readability seems to be the cloze procedure with some special modifications as suggested by Kane, Byrne, and Hater (1974). In this procedure every fifth word or math symbol is eliminated and replaced by a blank. When words are eliminated, the blanks are longer _____; when math symbols are eliminated, the blanks are shorter _____. Mathematical symbols are ordered according to the order of oral pronunciation, and each symbol is counted separately, e.g. $\geq$ counts as two symbols $>$, ___. Thus 4 = 8 x 1/2 is counted as 4, =, 8, x, 1, /, 2.

Informal reading inventories which assess the student's abilities to use the special reading skills which are appropriate for reading math is a second procedure which may be used to match learners with a particular text (Dupuis & Askov, 1982; Estes & Vaughan, 1977; O'Mara, 1981; Singer & Donlan, 1980).

General readability formulas which count sentences and syllables such as the Fry, Raygor, Smog, and Dale-Chall are not appropriate for matching learners with math textbooks. These formulas should only be used to distinguish texts which present difficult concepts in a simpler linguistic style from texts which present difficult concepts in a difficult linguistic style.

Kane, Byrne, and Hater (1974) have developed two readability formulas specifically for math texts. Both formulas are based on four hundred word samples for every thirty pages of text and use cloze scores as the criterion variable. Results are interpreted in terms of cloze scores which would be expected to be achieved by junior high students. Specific information regarding these two complicated formulas is available in the Kane, Byrne, and Hater text.

# Conclusions and Recommendations

It would seem that reading instruction as it applies to specific reading skills required to read math should be an integral aspect of mathematics instruction. The reading skills which are required differ significantly from those required for general reading, and since they are generally concerned with concept development and understanding the techniques for problem solving, the best person to provide skill instruction in this area is the regular mathematics instructor.

There is a significantly large body of research and literature which is available in the area of reading math, most notably in the areas of general problems, vocabulary or concept development, and problem solving of word problems. Much work remains to be done in several areas of mathematics instruction. Most existing research deals with general math and algebra, and there is need for research in the areas of geometry, trigonometry, and calculus. There is a need to continue the work on developing specialized readability formulas for math which was begun by Kane, Byrne, and Hater. Finally, there is a need for research (especially experimental design) which assesses the effectiveness of suggested strategies for promoting vocabulary development, interpreting literal meanings of math passages, and developing the special study skills which are required for math.

## Annotated Bibliography for Reading in Mathematics Instruction

Aiken, L. Mathematics as a creative language. *Arithmetic Teacher*, 1977, *24*, 241-246.
    Discusses general problems of mathematics language and suggests some strategies to relate math to ordinary life experiences of children.

Alabama State Department of Education. *Mathematics supplement to a miniguide to reading in the content area*, 1976. (ED 189 568)
    Discusses reading skills which should be developed concomitantly with fundamental math concepts. The report also suggests strategies to use to help students develop those skills.

Barney, L. Problems associated with the reading of arithmetic. *Arithmetic Teacher*, 1972, *19*, 131-133.
    Discusses problems associated with technical concepts, length of word problems, multiple meanings, and uses of punctuation and abbreviations.

Bye, M.P. *Reading in math and cognitive development.* Paper presented at the Transmountain Regional Conference of the International Reading Association, Alberta, 1975. (ED 124 926)
    Reports on a research study which suggests that problems in reading math may actually be due to the fact that a large percentage of high school students have not reached Piaget's formal operations stage. Presents good overview of Piagetian theory.

Byrne, M.A., & Mason, G.E. When pictures and words conflict. *Elementary School Journal*, 1976, *76*, 310-314.
A study which discovered that teachers' grading practices often discourage students from thinking through word problems on their own.

Campbell, A. How readability formulae fall short in matching student to text in the content area. *Journal of Reading*, 1979, *22*, 683-689.
Presents the problems in using general readability formulae to assess math texts and discusses five factors which influence the readability of math.

Ciani, A.J. Mastering word and symbol language in mathematics. *School Science and Mathematics*, 1981, *81*, 371-377.
Suggests a taxonomy of reading skills for math and strategies for developing reading skills at each level.

Cohen, S.A., & Stover, G. Effects of teaching sixth grade students to modify format variables of math word problems. *Reading Research Quarterly*, 1981, *16*, 175-200.
Reports on research in which gifted students rewrote word problems to make them easier for sixth grade math students and identifies the variables which make word problems difficult.

Cronnell, B. (Ed.). *Preliminary specifications of content for instruction in subject area vocabulary*. Southwest Regional Lab for Research and Development, 1977. (ED 172 140)
Gives lists of technical terms for use in vocabulary instruction in six subject areas for grades K-6 and reports on the steps taken to compile the lists.

Devine, T.G. Reading—study skills in mathematics. Paper presented at the International Reading Association Conference, Ireland, 1979. (ED 189 573)
Gives suggestions for teaching specialized study skills in math as well as a general strategy for solving word problems.

Dolgin, A.B. Improvement of mathematical learning through reading instruction. *High School Journal*, 1977, *61*, 59-69.
Article focuses on the necessity for high school math teachers to teach reading skills which are required to read math textbooks efficiently. Diagnostic procedures, readability problems, and math specific reading skills are addressed. Model lessons for developing comprehension and word meaning are presented along with techniques for assessing comprehension.

Dunlap, W.P., & McKnight, M.B. Vocabulary translation for conceptualizing math word problems. *Reading Teacher*, 1978, *32*, 182-189.
Describes a three level translation process for helping students to develop strategies to solve word problems in math.

Dupuis, M.M., & Askov, E.N. *Content area reading: An individualized approach*. Englewood Cliffs, New Jersey: Prentice-Hall, 1982.
Offers suggestions for teaching specific skills, selecting and evaluating materials, developing units of instruction, and dealing with exceptional learners and learners who are culturally and/or linguistically different. A cloze exercise for math teachers is included.

Earle, R.A. *Teaching reading and mathematics*. Newark, Delaware: International Reading Association, 1976.
Describes a four step hierarchy of reading skills for reading math, suggests teaching strategies for developing skills at each level, outlines a general procedure for attacking word problems, also gives a list of words which appear most frequently in math texts and a list of suggested high interest materials for math classrooms, grades 5-12.

Earp, N.W. Observations on teaching reading in mathematics. *Journal of Reading*, 1970, *13*, 529-533.
Reviews the research on the relationship between arithmetic and vocabulary knowledge and word problem solving ability.

Elliot, P.G., & Wiles, C.A. The print is part of the problem. *School Science and Mathematics*, 1980, *80*, 37-42.
Gives information on using the cloze procedure to establish the readability materials.

Estes, T.H., & Vaughan, J.L. *Reading and Learning in the content classroom*. Boston: Allyn & Bacon, 1978.

Florida State Department of Education. *Reading the language of mathematics*, 1975. (ED 134 972)
Offers comprehensive overview of reading and study skills needed for math and suggestions for promoting those skills and a bibliography of voluntary math reading materials.

Georgia State Department of Education. *Reading mathematics*, 1975. (ED 105 407)
Discusses the different types of eye movements which are required for reading math and problems with multiple meanings and word-symbol relationships.

Godfrey, M. How to develop the mathematics review lesson. *Reading Improvement*, 1979, *16*, 219-221.
Discusses the use of review lessons to review important concepts through problem analyses.

Hater, M.A., & Kane, R.B. The cloze procedrue as a measure of mathematical English. *Journal for Research in Mathematics Education*, 1975, *6*, 121-127.
Describes use of modified cloze procedure to determine the readability of math materials.

Henrichs, M., & Sisson, T. Mathematics and the reading process: A practical application of theory. *Mathematics Teacher*, 1980, *73*, 253-257.
Based on the involvement of a junior high math department in a content area reading program, this article lists important reading and study skills as well as techniques for developing skills.

Herber, H.L. *Teaching reading in the content area* (2nd ed.). Englewood Cliffs, New Jersey: Prentice-Hall, 1978.
Presents reading and reasoning guides for geometry.

Hollander, S.K. *Reading the special language of mathematics*. Paper presented at the Annual Convention of the International Reading Association, Miami Beach, May 1977.
Discusses difficulties inherent in reading math and suggests strategies to remediate difficulties.

Indiana State Department of Education. *Reading effectiveness programs: Middle, junior, and secondary school guides*, 1975. (ED 119 413)
Presents general concerns of reading in math and sample units of instruction employing strategies to develop reading skills in math.

Kane, R.B. The readability of mathematics textbooks revisited. *Mathematics Teacher*, 1970, *53*, 579-583.
States several reasons why readability formulas which count sentences and syllables are not really appropriate for math texts.

Kane, R.B., Byrne, M.A., & Hater, M.A. *Helping children read mathematics.* New York: American Book, 1974.
> Outlines steps for using the cloze procedure in math, presents two special formulas for assessing the readability of math texts, and presents a general overview of reading problems in math.

Knight, L.N., & Hargis, C.H. Math language ability: Its relationship to reading in math. *Language Arts,* 1977, *54,* 423-428.
> Discusses the relationship of one's knowledge of syntactic structure to one's ability to read math materials.

Koenke, K., & Monteith, M. *Reading instruction in the content area.* Eric Clearinghouse on Reading and Communication Skills, 1978. (ED 149 302)
> Provides resource guide and annotated bibliography for integrating reading in content area subjects.

Krulik, S. To read or not to read, that is the question. *Mathematics Teacher,* 1980, *73,* 248-252.
> Opts for reading in math as the answer to the question in the title and suggests strategies which can be used to develop the skills which are necessary.

Kruse, R.M. *A comparative study of the effectiveness of formal and informal teaching in science, math, and social studies,* 1979. (ED 183 394)
> A study to determine differences in vocabulary development when one teacher uses a formal plan for teaching vocabulary and another teacher teaches vocabulary only as the need arises with no formal system. The study found no significant differences in learner vocabulary development.

Leeds, D.S. Summary of research related to reading in the content areas—science and math. *Reading World,* 1970, *10,* 89-95.
> Discusses the use of modified language experience approach to middle school reading programs in the content areas.

Lees, F. Mathematics and reading. *Journal of Reading,* 1976, *19,* 621-626.
> Lees suggests that math achievement can be improved by improving the ability of students to read math materials. He discusses various diagnostic procedures including the cloze, IRA, standardized tests, and readability formulas. He also presents eight suggestions for improving comprehension, and discusses advisable procedures in assigning reading material.

Maffei, A.C. Mathematics in the language arts. *Elementary English,* 1975, *52,* 325-326.
> An overview of student problems in reading math, especially concerning words with multiple meanings.

Maffei, A.C. Reading analysis in mathematics. *Journal of Reading,* 1973, *16,* 546-549.
> Discusses the application of the PQ4R study formula to the solution of word problems in math classes.

Manzo, A.V. *The math student/the math teacher/the math problem.* Paper presented at the Annual Meeting of the Missouri Council of Teachers of Mathematics, 1975. (ED 114 767)
> Outlines the ReQuest procedure for teaching students to solve word problems. Teachers and students engage in mutual questioning concerning each sentence of the problem.

McCabe, P. *The effect upon comprehension of mathematics material repatterned on the basis of oral language.* Paper presented at the Annual Convention of the International Reading Association, Miami Beach, 1977. (ED 140 275)

Reports research in which repatterning word problems on the basis of students' oral language resulted in greater problem solving, and also isolates the factors which make word problems more difficult.

Morrison, B. *The identification of reading skills essential for learning in seven content areas at postelementary levels.* Technical Report #528. Wisconsin Research and Development Center for Individualized Schooling, 1980. (ED 185 536)

Reviews survey of sixty-five math teachers with an average of thirteen years experience in classroom teaching to determine the reading skills which they deem essential for reading math.

Munro, J. Language abilities and math performance. *Reading Teacher*, 1979, *32*, 900-915.

Discusses differences between general verbal statements and verbal statements in math and proposes teaching strategies to help students overcome problems in math.

O'Mara, D.A. The process of reading mathematics. *Journal of Reading*, 1981, *25*, 22-29.

A comprehensive, critical review of research in the areas of the language contexts of math, general reading ability, specific reading skills in math, and the readability of math materials. An excellent review of research.

Pachtman, A.B., & Riley, J.D. Teaching the vocabulary of mathematics through interaction, exposure, and structure. *Journal of Reading*, 1978, *22*, 240-244.

Outlines nine specific steps necessary to develop a structured overview of vocabulary in math and gives sample overviews for integers and mathematical operations.

Riley, J.D., & Pachtman, A.B. Reading math word problems: Telling them what to do is not telling them how to do it. *Journal of Reading*, 1978, *21*, 531-534.

Outlines specific steps for developing a three level reading guide to help students through the process of attacking word problems.

Robinson, H.A. *Teaching reading and study strategies: The content areas.* Boston: Allyn & Bacon, 1975.

Chapter eight suggests strategies for math teachers for developing vocabulary, concepts, principles, rules, graphic interpretations, and problem solving.

Rubens, P. *Decoding the calculus: Double jeopardy in readability.* Paper presented at the Annual Convention of the International Reading Association, St. Louis, 1980. (ED 188 120)

Reports on a study in which a math teacher with little reading background instructs one group of learners in problem solving, and a reading teacher with little math background instructs a different but matched group. Results indicate that those learners instructed by the reading teacher became better word problem solvers.

Schell, V.J. *Learning partners: Reading and mathematics.* Paper presented at a meeting of the Missouri State Council of the International Reading Association, 1981. (ED 199 564)

An overview of specialized reading skills required in math and suggested teaching techniques.

Shepherd, D.L. *Comprehensive high school reading methods* (3rd ed.). Columbus, Ohio: Charles E. Merrill, 1982.

Chapter twelve presents an overview of reading skills which are required in math and suggests strategies to develop those skills.

Singer, S., & Donlan, D. *Reading and learning from text.* Boston: Little, Brown, 1980.
Chapter fourteen presents an overview of problems typically encountered in reading math and suggested strategies and study formulas.

Skrypa, A. *Effects of mathematical vocabulary training on problem solving abilities of third and fourth graders.* Unpublished doctoral dissertation, Rutgers University, 1979. (ED 172 169)
Suggests that teaching math vocabulary can increase problem solving ability as measured by the Stanford Diagnostic Test of math achievement.

Stover, G. Rewording arithmetic problems for sixth and eighth graders to minimize reading difficulties. *Reading Improvement,* 1980, *17,* 26-35.
Identifies variables which contribute to student difficulties in solving word problems and suggests steps to rewrite problems to make them easier.

Sullivan, K. *The comprehension of mathematical language: A communication approach.* Paper presented at the American Reading Forum Conference, 1980. (ED 197 287)
Attempts to increase comprehension by classifying mathematical terms as either matter or relational terms and suggests strategies for teaching using this approach.

Texas Education Agency. *Learning partners: Reading and mathematics,* 1979. (ED 179 422)
Gives an overview of important skills for reading math, suggests sample activities for skill development, and provides lists of teacher resources and voluntary reading materials.

Thelen, J.N. Just because kids can't read doesn't mean that they can't learn or every science and math teacher is not a teacher of reading. *School Science and Mathematics,* 1979, *79,* 457-463.
Focuses on the use of advance organizers to promote concept development, lists steps in preparing an advance organizer and provides examples.

Thomas, E.L., & Robinson, H.A. *Improving reading in every class: A sourcebook for teachers* (2nd ed.). Boston: Allyn & Bacon, 1977.
Focuses on the development of special guide sheets to help students overcome reading problems such as vocabulary and word problems.

Wesley, E.N., & Tanner, F.W. Mathematics and language. *Arithmetic Teacher,* 1980, *28,* 32-34.
Discusses three elements related to reading in math (language, vocabulary, and readability) and makes suggestions for improvements.

# Reading in the Content Area of Music

Bernard J. Badiali
*Gateway Regional High School*
*Woodbury Heights, New Jersey*

## Overview

Tragically, when budget cuts occur, they often occur in music departments. Perhaps, if music were more closely linked to basic skills, such as mathematics and reading, there would be a stronger rationale to look in other areas of the curriculum to make those dreaded cuts (Klotman, 1977). Unfortunately, many music teachers regard themselves more as musicians than teachers (Tellstrom, 1978). Music teachers may feel uncomfortable incorporating the teaching of reading skills into their weekly lessons. Chances are, however, that good music teachers already provide students with some essential reading skills. There seems to be extensive common ground between reading language and reading music. Maybe it is past time for them to be linked more closely (Tucker, 1980). Much of the literature written since 1976 addresses the issue of how valuable it is to link music and reading.

## Research

There is a comparative scarcity of research linking reading and music (Tucker, 1980). Some early empirical findings (1943-1971) have been interpreted to indicate a highly positive correlation between reading and music (Zinar, 1976). Still other assessments of these studies refute this conclusion (Groff, 1977). The latter assessment suggests that, based on the early studies which dealt directly with the effects of music instruction on reading development, it is inappropriate to advise music teachers that their instruction is a valuable aid to the language/reading teacher. The second view holds that there has been little conclusive evidence to support or reject the notion that music instruction does affect reading development (Groff, 1977). This latter view is supported by Wooderson (1977a, 1978). Wooderson's research suggests that in beginning reading instruction music may have positive effects on attitude, but no significant effect on reading skill attainment is noted. Wooderson catalogs the music methods texts which advocate integrating music and language arts (1977a:3), but she concludes that "these worthy recommendations are seldom investigated within the rigors of experimental research" (1977a:4).

## Skills

While the difference of opinion continues, it does seem obvious that learning music is somewhat similar to learning language. Both tasks depend on the student's ability to perceive likenesses and differences in sounds, shapes, and symbols. Reading words and reading music are both done left to right and top to bottom. Reading musical notations may be easier than reading alphabets since, unlike letters, notes are constant with the sounds they represent. Figure 1 illustrates how some music activities can help develop abilities for reading language (Lloyd, 1978).

Figure 1. Music Activities for Helping Develop and Reinforce Specific Abilities for Language Reading.

| General area | Ability related to reading | Musical activity to reinforce ability |
|---|---|---|
| Auditory reception | Hearing spoken language | Hearing music sounds |
| Auditory discrimination | Ability to distinguish between spoken sounds in sentences, words, letters | Practice in recognizing sounds made with instruments, voice, clapping, etc. |
| | | Practice identifying where a sound is coming from, pitch, intensity, etc. |
| | | Isolating which instruments are playing when two or three are playing together |
| Auditory association | Ability to interpret spoken sounds and related concepts presented orally | Practice repeating rhythmic patterns by clapping, stamping, etc. |

Figure 1
(continued)

| General area | Ability related to reading | Musical activity to reinforce ability |
|---|---|---|
| | | Memorizing songs, then singing notes in sequence |
| | | Remembering which sound comes next in a melody |
| Visual reception | Seeing letters, words, pictures | Seeing musical notes and instruments |
| Visual discrimination | Seeing difference between graphic representations of letters and words | Practice discriminating different graphic representations of notes for time and tone values |
| Visual association | Realizing that words and letters are written forms of language and sound | Practice associating specific notes with specific sounds and time values |
| | | Reading notes and translating them into actions, rhythms, tunes |
| Visual sequential memory | Ability to remember sounds and words long enough to obtain meaning | Practice remembering tunes and song words in order to play and sing them |
| | | Copying music, song sheets |
| Eye-motor coordination | Ability to track visually from left to right and top to bottom of page | Practice in following music sheets from left to right and top to bottom |
| Form constancy | Recognizing that a word spelt in capitals, lower case, and cursive is always the same word | Practice finding notes of the same time value, even when they are of different colors |
| | | Finding notes of the same pitch when they have different time values |
| | | Recognizing that felt notes used to make tunes have the same value as notes drawn on music sheets |
| Figure ground | Recognizing that distracting marks on a page are not essential to the reading process | Practice associating the sound of a note with its graphic representation |
| Language reception | Ability to listen to and understand spoken language | Practice listening to and understanding songs and explanations of musical activities |

(from Lloyd, 1978, p. 324)

Despite the differences of opinion concerning the research of the past linking music and reading, it is our view that one can facilitate the other. Music is ideal for developing adequate oral language through songs. Listening and other music-related language skills are crucial in developing readiness for reading (Reeves, 1978). Building basic skills through music instruction can provide many students with the motivation they need to learn how to read. All music teachers should consider capitalizing on student interests in order to help them acquire better reading skills.

## Strategies

It has been suggested that music specialists should learn ways in which music can be used to reinforce or enhance learning in other subjects (Reeves, 1978). Music can be used easily with the language experience approach. Writing words to songs is comparable to writing poetry (Reeves, 1978). Lyric analysis of new compositions or popular recordings can facilitate comprehension and provide unique motivation for reading practice. All children have a need to express themselves through music (Zinar, 1976).

"Translating Latin into Music," Schenkman (1979) discusses various esoteric and practical strategies for combining the reading of music with the reading of language. He draws logical parallels between the concept of syntax in music and language. He suggests a wealth of strategies for combining music with linguistic vocabulary and research skills.

A major resource for linking music and reading is television. In a study which used musical television to teach reading, there were significantly positive results (Hirst & O'Such, 1979). The lyrics of musical jingles from commercials were used to teach various reading skills. Since children generally spend more time watching television than going to school, associating viewing with reading practice could have lasting carryover effects on reading ability.

## Conclusion

Finally, it must be said that there is a need for more research describing the exact nature of the relationship between reading music and reading language. All educators, but especially music teachers, have a stake in identifying such a relationship. Only through valid field research can we identify the attributes that connect reading and music.

Certainly, only through close cooperation between the music teacher and the reading specialist can we make progress toward discovering this relationship.

## Annotated Bibliography for
## Reading in Music

Brown, M.H. Time for music. *Music Teacher*, 1977, *10*, 15-16.
>Presents progress report on the use of multimedia materials. The author reports on the success of this primary school reading program involving materials developed by the project "Music Education of Young Children" sponsored by the School's Council Project.

Groff, P. The effect of music on reading. *Reading Horizons*, 1976, *2*, 20-24.
>Suggests that teachers of reading would be in error to suppose that the displacement of regular methods of reading instruction in their classes by music activities will produce exceptional gains in skills.

Groff, P. Reading music affects reading language? Says Who? *Music Educator's Journal*, 1977, *1*, 37-41.
>Reviews research literature which refutes the notion that music and reading are related. The author suggests that there is no substantial evidence to prove that teaching music helps language reading and it is inappropriate to advise music teachers that their instruction is a valuable aid to the efforts of the language reading teacher.

Hirst, L.T., & O'Such, T. Using musical television commercials to teach reading. *Teaching Exceptional Children*, 1979, *11*, 80-81.
>Suggests that teachers take advantage of the time children spend watching TV. The authors summarize a successful classroom practice that uses television commercials to help remediate slow readers.

Klotman, R.H. When you go back to basics, take music along. *Music Educator's Journal*, 1977, *9*, 77.
>Urges teachers to link music to reading and promote it to avoid cutting school music programs. Since music can be linked to creative expression it has many uses in reading.

Lloyd, M. Teaching music to aid beginning readers. *Reading Teacher*, 1978, *32*, 323-327.
>Reading both music and language depend on similar skills. The author compares skills in each area and suggests ways to combine reading and music on the elementary level.

Plummeridge, C. The reading project: Observations. *Music Teacher*, 1978, 9, 15-16.
>Critique of "Time for Music," a multimedia kit developed by the Schools Council Project called "Music Education for Young Children." The author takes exception to earlier review which describes these materials favorably.

Reeves, H.R. Building basic skills with music. *Music Educator's Journal*, 1978, *9*, 75.
>Music can be used in developing listening and language skills in elementary schools. The author suggests methods for teaching auditory discrimination and concept development through song lyrics. She suggests that oral language development is crucial in developing readiness for reading.

Schenkman, W. Language, music, musical language, or translating Latin into music. *American Music Teacher*, 1979, *9*, 14-17.
Examines the relationship between Latin and music. Suggests a significant connection between the two subjects, whereby the study of the one might well influence and advance the study of another.

Tellstrom, A. Annual report. *Music Educator's Journal*, 1978, *65*, 66-73.

Tucker, A. Music and the teaching of reading: A review of the literature. *Reading Improvement*, 1981, 14-19.
A review of research and opinion which concludes that there is a scarcity of research linking reading and music. The author suggests more research be done in this area.

Tucker, A. Reading and music: Can we bring them together? *Reading Improvement*, 1980, *F*, 224-225.
Points out that music can be tool for enhancing reading instruction, then the teachers of music and the teachers of reading would do well to articulate mutual concerns and methods. When there is a deliberate attempt to put these subjects together, there is a greater chance for student success.

Wooderson, D.C. *The effect of musical and nonmusical media on word reading.* Doctoral dissertation, Florida State University, August 1977.

Wooderson, D.C. The effect of using a worksheet in teaching music reading to fourth grade students. *PMEA Bulletin of Research in Music Education*, 1977, *8*, 12-14.

Wooderson, D.C. The effect of specific music activities on elementary language arts. *PMEA Bulletin of Research in Music Education*, 1978, *9*, 30-32.
Offers a series of research studies focusing on the relationship between music and beginning reading achievement. Her conclusions do not support a causative relationship, although students like the reading/music combinations.

Zinar, R. Reading language and reading music: Is there a connection? *Music Educator's Journal, 1976, 3*, 70-74.
Reviews the research that finds a positive correlation between reading music and reading language. Music is seen to act as a motivational tool as well as a means through which reading-related skills are acquired. The author suggests that the connection between music and reading is only one of many practical applications where the arts have been useful in helping learners attain basic skills.

# Reading in the Content Area of Physical Education and Health

Bernard J. Badiali
*Gateway Regional High School*
*Woodbury Heights, New Jersey*

## Overview

Although the areas of health, physical education, and recreation are thought of as activity or laboratory classes, they still offer strong possibilities for content area reading. It's important for students to associate words and concepts with mental and physical experiences. Subject areas like health and physical education provide excellent settings to accomplish reading objectives where other content areas may not. Student interest in sports is high. That interest can be channeled in specific ways in order to improve reading.

## Research

While there hasn't been much published concerning reading as it relates to health and physical education, there are enough sources available to serve as a guide for any teacher in these areas. The pattern in most of the available literature is the same. Principles of teaching reading are presented to content teachers using examples and terminology appropriate to their disciplines. Suggested activities are grouped in the areas of readiness, comprehension, vocabulary, and study skills. The literature will not only be of practical use to the content area teachers, it will also serve as an aid to reading specialists who wish to coordinate activities with those teachers.

## Skills

Reading isn't often thought of as a motor skill. The fact is, however, that reading is a kind of physical as well as mental activity. Developing prereading skills in the elementary schools can be very important to a student's reading readiness. Activities like skipping, balancing on one foot, and hand-eye coordination exercises can be valuable to pre- and beginning readers (Florida, 1975). There is a kind of parallel between an athlete training to compete and a reader training to read (Gentile, 1980).

Some programs suggest that individualized instruction can continue readiness past the primary grades in the form of read-and-do exercises. For example, learning stations in the gymnasium or an all-purpose room could accommodate small groups. Written instructions for a child to perform a basic task might read:

Do these exercises at your own pace.

Read *The Tumbler's Manual.*

Do a forward roll, page 10.

Do a backward roll, page 18.

Exercises like this reinforce the physical as well as the reading skills involved. They provide practice and they can help diagnose readiness in both areas.


## Strategies

Teaching reading comprehension is discussed in the literature more in terms of activities than in terms of diagnosis. Although there are examples of modified cloze techniques using sports as a topic, they are used to provide practice rather than to establish how appropriate materials are matched to readers. The use of informal reading inventories seems inappropriate for physical education, but could be used with various health textbooks.

Several sources included activities which address various levels of comprehension. Exercises which provide practice in listening comprehension as well as written levels of comprehension were included (Alabama, 1976a). Skills like summarizing, critical thinking, and understanding relevant information also are discussed. One source provided many examples as well as teacher guides using various sports games as topics (Estes & Vaughan, 1978).

An excellent way to assess and deal with student comprehension is through the use of a three level study guide. Following almost any piece of reading students could be asked questions on the literal, inferential, and applicative levels. A good example of this technique is used in a senior high health unit (Peters, 1980).

Level I—What did the author say?
Example_____ Pregnancy begins with conception and ends with childbirth (labor) or abortion (miscarriage).

Level II—Check those items that are "correct" interpretations of reading assignment.
Example_____ Pregnant women have a responsibility toward their unborn children.

Level III—Check those items that you think best apply.
Example_____ Pregnancy changes all things.

Sports has its own specialized vocabulary. Since many students enjoy sports, they are motivated to learn the meanings of new words. The informed physical education teacher will stress not only the words and their meanings but also the process for learning new words. What is more, teachers in almost any subject area can use sports vocabulary to motivate other kinds of learning.

One source suggested using the Winter Olympics for teaching reading throughout an entire school. English and social studies classes could use the names of the Olympians in a unit on name characteristics or a unit on abbreviations. Mathematics classes could focus on the metric system or on comparing scores and times of events. Science classes could easily tie in the making of charts and graphs whose process could later be transferred to more specific content (Peters, 1980). Obviously the teacher of physical education could use any or all of these topics through which to teach reading.

Generally, any sports news clipping can be appropriate for studying vocabulary and for asking comprehension questions on several levels (Gentile, 1980a). An excellent way for a physical education teacher to teach and reinforce vocabulary is through a one-page handout which summarizes a lesson. All key vocabulary should be capitalized. Questions could be included on the back of such a summary.

Health and physical education teachers can create interesting and informative vocabulary bulletin boards. One source suggests various places to which a teacher can write for free bulletin board materials (Maring & Ritson, 1980). There are other sources for teaching vocabulary with example crossword puzzles using word lists specifically developed for these content areas (Alabama, 1976b).

There is even a miniguide on driver safety designed to help the driver education teacher understand and teach the reading process with special emphasis on specific vocabulary for drivers (Alabama, 1976a).

Examples from physical education are also included throughout each source (Florida, 1975). The following sample is from an exercise on context clues.

Directions: Fill in the missing words.
The _____ plays directly _____ the center and handles the _____ every play.
The fullback is _____ him with the left _____ three long steps to his left.
The _____ halfback plays just _____ his own end and close to the line of _____.

Most of the books and articles which treat content area reading in physical education and health make clear that they are just intended as guides for practicing teachers. Once content teachers understand the principles involved in teaching reading, they can easily adapt some portions of their own lessons. The literature suggests the use of student questionnaires to determine learning styles (Alabama, 1976b). Student guided learning centers may be desirable for portions of the curriculum.

Various units in sports involve games that demand rigid organization. Learning to play these games is an organizational skill and can be taught that way. Furthermore, it can be transferred to other content areas (Estes & Vaughan, 1978). Even reference skills can be taught through physical education. Understanding and utilizing the library can be a part of any unit in physical education. For example, the student could be given a "treasure hunt" in the library to locate answers on a sports quiz. Questions like: "Who won the World Series for the past five years?" could be asked to guide the students through various reference books in the library.

Although there hasn't been much specific information published concerning teaching reading in physical education and health, there is more than enough to get willing teachers started. Working the time in for reading in any content area may seem difficult at first but if teachers are committed, they will find a way. An easy way to begin a reading program could be to start a lending library in the locker room. Collect sports paperbacks that will hold high interest for young athletes and devise an easy way to manage their borrowing (Maring & Ritson, 1980).

## Conclusion

While physical education and reading may not seem as companionable as some other academic areas, there is much they can do together to facilitate better reading skills. There is a need for field research which can better describe the relationship between the two areas. A closer articulation between the reading specialist and physical education teacher could only succeed in attaining each one's goal—a more competent learner.

## Annotated Bibliography for
## Reading in Physical Education and Health

Alabama State Department of Education. A miniguide to reading in the content area of driver and traffic safety education. Montgomery: Division of Instructional Services, 1976.

Designed to help the driver education teacher understand the reading process. Gives suggestions for implementing reading instruction and for identifying the reading skills that a student will need in order to become proficient in the area of driver education. Recognition of words is the primary concern of the first part of the document, and specific vocabulary development activities center on lists of essential vocabulary words for drivers. Methods for presenting these words are suggested. Also included are a sample lesson on teaching with a film, activities related to driver education designed to develop study skills, and methods of making assignments to students.

Alabama State Department of Education. How to reinforce reading through health, physical education, and recreation. Montgomery: Division of Instructional Services, 1976.

Intended for use in inservice workshops for health and physical education teachers, this guide contains suggestions designed to help these teachers integrate the teaching of reading skills into their curricula. Sample activities are provided to demonstrate how the physical education teacher can use different methods and strategies to help students extend their vocabularies and reinforce their reading comprehension. Suggested activities include games and puzzles; working with lists of frequently used and rarely used words; finding hidden and missing words; developing visual recognition and comprehension; and learning special archery terms. A checklist of study skills, a teaching model for beginning volleyball, and a sample test are also included.

Estes, T.H., & Vaughan, J.L., Jr. *Reading and learning in the content classroom*. Boston: Allyn & Bacon, 1978.

Concerns both diagnostic and instructional techniques in content area instruction. Provides content area teachers with the skills needed to diagnose reading and learning difficulties. Prescribes learning environments as well as diagnostic and prescriptive insights for teachers.

Florida State Department of Education. Physical education and reading: A winning team. Tallahassee, 1975.

Acquaints physical education teachers with the meanings of some terms used in reading that are related to physical education, acquaints physical education teachers with reading skills that can be taught or reinforced through physical education activities, provides a source or model of such activities, and assists reading teachers in relating reading skills to physical education. Suggested activities are grouped in the areas of readiness, comprehension, decoding, reference and study skills, and diagnosis. Examples of sensorimotor activities listed under readiness include locating parts of the body, balancing on one foot, skipping, and coordinating eye/hand and foot/eye movements. It is suggested that these activities be used by teachers in physical education and reading classes at all levels, to assist students in upgrading their reading skills.

Gentile, L.M. *Using sports and physical education to strengthen reading skills.* Newark, Delaware: International Reading Association, 1980.
Gives an overview of reading for coaches and physical education teachers, samples of reading activities for their classes, and procedures for readability testing and evaluation of teaching materials. A good bibliography of readings for students in various sports is included.

Gentile, L.M. Using sports to strengthen content area reading skills, *Journal of Reading*, 1980, *24*, 245-248.
Suggests using materials dealing with sports in a variety of ways in content classes to improve reading and critical thinking. Provides specific suggestions for using sports in English, mathematics, social studies, science, and health classes.

Maring, G.H., & Ritson, R. Reading improvement in the gymnasium. *Journal of Reading*, 1980, *24*, 27-31.
Suggests ten teaching strategies for combining reading skills development and physical education instruction.

Peters, F.J.J. The 1980 olympics: A schoolwide TV - reading project. *Journal of Reading*, 1980, *23*, 300-304.
Suggests that televised broadcasts of the 1980 Olympics can provide teachers with material for reading and other classes.

# Reading in the
# Content Area of Science

Sarah D. Weidler
*Pennsylvania State University*

## Overview

This report summarizes the findings of a review of the literature in the area of science and reading since 1975 and includes an annotated bibliography for each citation. The literature describing research or theoretically slanted articles is initially introduced, while the more practical articles stressing skills and strategies for the classroom teacher follow.

## Research/Theory

Articles concerning research and theory in the combined areas of reading and science are surprisingly scanty in number. All describe a different area of research related to science; there does not appear to be a common denominator.

A theoretical article by Eisenberg (1977) concerned the structure of the language in regard to science, and how the various aspects of language (lexical, syntactic, semantic, and logical) affect comprehension and ease of reading. According to Eisenberg, there is a vocabulary common to the sciences, a lexicon consisting of terms which are nonambiguous. This consistent vocabulary includes words which have one and only one meaning in the science context. Such a lexical feature of science language structure should prove advantageous to students since only one definition of a term is appropriate. However, it is suggested that a study of the differences between word meanings be encouraged both in and out of science contexts.

In addition, science often presents information as a cause-effect relationship, promoting causal chaining patterns which can be deleterious to comprehension. Note the following example of a causal chaining pattern:

> The water thundering over the spillway possesses kinetic energy, which is converted to mechanical energy as it turns the blades of the turbine at the foot of the waterfall. The generator converts the mechanical energy to electrical energy, which is used to light a bulb, which in turn gives off light energy. In this process, some of the electrial energy is also converted to heat. (Eisenberg, 1977:6)

The amount of anaphora (omitted words the reader must infer) certainly contributes to comprehension difficulties. In the above example, "which" and "it" represent different forms of energy in different sentences requiring the reader to follow and infer such changes in meaning sequentially in the context.

Passive verbs, embedded sentences, and nominalizations are also prevalent in scientific writing, all of which make comprehension more difficult than their counterparts: active verbs, nonembedded sentences, and transformations.

Eisenberg suggests that instruction in the format of such syntactic features as causal chaining may prove useful for students in preparation for notetaking from science texts or lectures. Teachers preparing to rewrite science materials will aim to eliminate passive verb tenses and embedded sentences, and to lessen the amount of anaphora in order to improve student comprehension.

Semantically and logically, science discourse is expository in nature and reflects a written rather than verbal domain. Scientific language is often terse and exact, using few examples or explanations. Essentially, much scientific writing lacks the redundancy necessary for immediate comprehension. Keeping this in mind, when scientific material is prepared it would be advantageous to include more concrete examples and explanations for the reader.

It would appear that attention to and appropriate adaptation of the lexical, syntactic, semantic, and logical features of scientific discourse could provide a more comprehensible base for the science student.

Several of the remaining theoretical articles were specific to the area of biology. Middleton (1978) investigated the possibility of predicting a student's reading ability, general science ability, or text readability when given only two of the three variables. Of particular interest was the conclusion that the Fry readability graph did accurately predict the readability levels of the selected biology textbooks. Wright (1980) found that high school students using biology materials written at a lower readability did not comprehend significantly more than students using the assigned biology text. Furukawa (1980) described the use of a cognitive processing capacity model (CPC) to help students organize themselves for learning and found the technique to be effective. A study conducted by Ricker (1978) compared natural and general science ability of junior high students to biology text readability and found significance among several of the variables.

Only one study pertained to elementary age students. Kruse (1979) addressed differences in teaching style (formal/informal) and found no significant differences in achievement. One final study conducted by Ley, Henry, and Rowsey (1979) hypothesized that general reading ability, problem-solving reading and thinking skills, and mathematical computation skills are related positively to performance when solving science related word problems. However, results suggested that students operate ineffectively when analyzing relationships within science word problems. The authors contend that content teachers should accept the responsibility to teach students the essential reading/thinking skills necessary for successful interpretation of specific content material.

After reviewing the research in the area of science and reading, it would appear that the following areas lend themselves to further research. Elementary school programs in relation to reading and science need serious study. Other specific science-related subjects, aside from biology, should be considered, such as chemistry and physics. Research relating to the structure of scientific discourse should be extended to investigate what features of scientific language cause the greatest problem and what types of teaching procedures are useful in helping students handle scientific writing successfully.

## Skills/Strategies

In content classrooms, the use of science texts predominates, even though many teachers realize that a single text does not necessarily suit every student. Many of the authors included in the bibliography have acknowledged the importance of text/student ability matching and recommend the use of the cloze procedure and informal reading inventories (IRI) for assessment. Carter and Simpson (1978) give practical suggestions for finding suitable materials and determining readability. Also included are sample questions for an IRI. Davis (1977) discusses application of reading expectancy and readability formulas so that alternate materials and instruction can be adopted. The Georgia

State Department of Education (1976) has released a guide which describes specific activities useful for ascertaining reading levels. Holliday and Braun (1979) include a discussion of readability scales applicable to science texts and also describe other textual elements which affect readability levels. Johnson's (1980) booklet includes two pages specific to science and contains instructions on preparing a cloze or maze assessment. Kennedy (1979) specifically applies the Fry readability scale to biology texts. Putnam (1979) recommends techniques useful for determining a student's instructional level and matching text material to that level, while Shuman (1978) describes use of the cloze procedure to determine readability. Shymansky and Yore (1979) present several readability methods and their variability. The Texas Education Agency (1981) includes sections in its publication concerning the determination of student reading level with an IRI, cloze, and the San Diego Quick Assessments. Thelen's monograph (1976) devotes part of a chapter to readability application. Van Duren (1979) describes the use of the cloze procedure for text selection and Wright (1980) also describes material selection techniques.

When discussing text assessment techniques, vocabulary and comprehension development are usually included in the same breath. There is no denying the need for concept/vocabulary load determination and instruction as well as attention to comprehension efficiency. Activities and suggestions for vocabulary and comprehension development were highly visible and detailed in a number of articles.

Various study strategies useful for science material were also addressed. Advance organizers, structured overviews, and study guides prepared by the teacher help prime students prior to instruction or reading by structuring concepts and vocabulary necessary for comprehension. Other related study skills for students include: setting purposes for reading and using survey techniques (SQ3R), as well as outlining, diagramming, notetaking, and test taking.

Barrow (1978) describes activities useful to the biology teacher to improve reading abilities of students, while Blake (1975) provides an overview of teaching techniques for various reading skills. Carter and Simpson (1978) suggest activities for vocabulary development and list three levels of comprehension useful for science teachers. David's article (1978) describes a workshop conducted with secondary science teachers in which specific reading/study skills were identified, and Davis (1977) provides a practical guide for the classroom teacher by including science topic suggestions to help improve reading.

The Georgia State Department of Education's (1976) guide cites specific activities for promoting reading skills at all levels. Johnson's

(1980) booklet provides information for administration of a directed reading activity in science and contains instructions on preparing a structured overview and applying mapping techniques. Kaplan and Tuchman (1980) list five strategies that foster independent learning of content area vocabulary, while Karahalios (1979) defines an advance organizer and describes its use in an experimental setting. Keimig (1976) examines a system for integrating reading into the earth science curriculum (SIRCA) and finds reaction to be positive. Manzo's article (1980) suggests three strategies to help students understand concepts in science-related material. Miceli (1975) describes an experimental program conducted in a junior high school which incorporated science vocabulary in all content areas. The results appeared favorable. Morrison (1980) designed a questionnaire to give content area teachers an opportunity to review skills necessary for vocabulary development, comprehension of written material, and efficient use of study time. The skills necessary for learning in the area of science are included.

Putnam's guide (1979) recommends developing vocabulary through context clues and the use of Latin and Greek roots, and developing main ideas through study guides. Shuman (1978) recommends a group approach to untangling sentence structure and teaching techniques for specialized vocabulary. The Texas Education Agency's publication (1981) provides tips on improving student reading skills and notetaking techniques, as well as strategies for test-taking and questioning strategies to improve comprehension. Thelen (1976) provides an informal study skills inventory in her monograph, and Wright (1980) discusses diagnosis of reading skills, reading skill development, and instructional planning.

Several articles discuss questioning strategies in regard to comprehending science-related reading. Both Lamb (1976) and Perry (1979) stress the importance of asking high-level types of questions to improve comprehension. Lamb also includes an extensive reference list for further reading. Two other articles, both by Leonard and Lowery (1976, 1978) describe a question assessment instrument useful for the teacher when selecting a text for science.

Also included are several miscellaneous articles which continue to address practical issues. Two are concerned with readability techniques and their shortcomings: Ricker (1978) discusses several readability formulas (Fry, FOG, SMOG) useful for text assessment, but also details other factors to be considered when assessing readability of science material. Nelson (1978) also lists factors beyond the quantitative ones most readability formulas use that should prove useful when judging readability.

Each of the following articles addresses a separate area: Cochran (1979) provides the classroom teacher with a "how to" guide describing the preparation of science reading kits. Cornett (1975) describes the successful incorporating of a sustained silent reading program in a ninth grade science classroom. Collins (1979) introduces a self-checking technique to assess a student's test taking and study attitudes. Criscuolo (1977) describes a program which uses biology as a base for developing interest in reading for sixth graders. Warren (1975) outlines the preparation of audio tapes and packets for poor readers in science. Esler and King (1979), by using manipulative and observational science activities as a stimulus, developed language experience stories used in both reading and language arts programs in a junior high school. Yore and Quinn (1977) recognize that students need to acquaint themselves with graphics prior to reading science material. They elaborate on specific procedures.

## Conclusion

A number of tested strategies are available to teachers in science and reading. The common techniques in science/reading involve concept learning, using advance organizers and concept labels (vocabulary), a concern for reading level of texts, using study guides, and process-oriented self-study procedures. Science teachers can test out the techniques to find ones which work for their content and students.

### Annotated Bibliography for Reading in Science Instruction

Ankeny, P., & McClurg, P. Testing Manzo's guided reading procedure. *Reading Teacher*, 1981, *34*, 681-685.
    Describes the use of Manzo's guided reading procedure (GRP) with fourth and fifth graders in social studies and science. The procedure consists of 1) purpose set: students are instructed to remember all they can and to shut their eyes after reading; 2) the teacher asks the class to tell everything they remember and the results are recorded on the blackboard; 3) students should locate missing items and correct them; 4) students are then to organize the information logically; 5) the teacher asks synthesizing questions to aid comprehension; 6) a conventional test is administered to test short term memory; and 7) another test is administered at a later date to assess long term memory. Students participating in the science experimental group showed no significant differences in retention.

Barrow, L.H. Close encounters of biology and reading. *American Biology Teacher*, 1978, *45*, 18-21.
    Describes what the biology teacher can do to improve the reading abilities of students, especially those at a frustration level.

Blake, S. *Teaching reading skills through social studies and science materials*, 1975. (ED 123 564)

For each of the subject areas, this manual provides an overview, a list of teaching techniques for the various reading skills, and model lessons. An appendix indicates reading materials suitable for both subjects, and a brief bibliography lists references.

Carter, G.S., & Simpson, R.D. Science and reading: A basic duo. *Science Teacher*, 1978, *45*, 19-21.

Gives practical suggestions for finding suitable material and determining readability. Sample questions are given for an Informal Group Reading Inventory. Activities are suggested for vocabulary development. Three levels of comprehension are discussed, and a chart of science processes with corresponding reading skills is given.

Cochran, C. Science reading kits. *Science and Children*, 1979, *17*, 12-13.

Offers "how to" guide describing the preparation of science reading kits. Students actually prepared the kits as science projects. Contents of kits included: books, articles, filmstrips, models, task cards, vocabulary, and spelling exercises. A solar heating science reading kit is described in detail.

Collins, M. Helping students do better on tests. *American Biology Teacher*, 1979, *41*, 239-240.

Describes a technique (self-checking key) which should prove useful to students. The key assesses a student's test taking and study attitudes. Directions and the actual "key" are included.

Cornett, C.F. Reading for fun...in science class? *Science Teacher*, 1975, *42*, 58-59.

Describes the incorporation of a free reading period in a ninth grade science classroom. The students were encouraged to read purely for enjoyment; no grades were involved. A list of books and magazines at various levels of readability and interest is provided.

Criscuolo, W.P. Centering in on books and life sciences. *Teacher*, 1977, *94*, 82-85.

Describes a year long program in a sixth grade classroom which used biology as a base for developing interest in reading. Assorted science centers are detailed. Lists of reference materials are also provided.

David, A.P. A science teacher, a reading teacher? A workshop with answers. *Science Education*, 1978, *62*, 181-186.

Describes a workshop conducted with more than twenty secondary science teachers. The workshop was concerned with the following: 1) teachers should learn that content texts are written in a technical manner, therefore, students need to be acquainted with the text's parts; 2) specific reading/study skills should be identified which are critical to the subject; 3) word recognition skills should be emphasized to encourage teacher competency; 4) teachers should be able to apply reading expectancy and readability formulas so that alternate materials and instruction can be adopted; 5) teachers should become acquainted with free and inexpensive materials available for instruction; and 6) teachers should be able to demonstrate a reading/study plan to their students.

Davis, J.B. Improving reading and the teaching of science. *Clearing House*, 1977, *50*, 390-392.

Offers a practical guide which includes suggestions for reading improvement by using science topics. Topics include: 1) improving students' reading of laboratory instructions; 2) improving comprehension through reading assignments; 3) improving vocabulary; and 4) improving student textbook studying. All descriptions are quite brief.

Eisenberg, A. *Lexical, syntactic, and semantic characterisitics of the language of science,* 1977. (ED 149 289)

Suggests that scientific discourse is difficult to read because of its lexical, syntactic, semantic, and logical features. Lexical features include: highly specialized vocabulary, uniformity of terms, and use of nontechnical terms with technical meanings. Syntactic features include: heavy use of passive form, information presented in the form of cause-effect, extensive causal chaining, and use of anaphora. Semantic features include: the absence of narrative voice, avoidance of figurative language and humor, and sparing use of examples and explanations. Logical features include: switching the reader from prose to numerical and nonnumerical symbolism, and the discourse being essentially a written, rather than verbal, language.

Esler, W.K., & King, M. Teaching reading through science experience stories. *School Science and Mathematics,* 1979, *76,* 203-206.

Using manipulative and observational science activities as a stimulus, science experience stories were developed and used in reading and language arts programs with remedial junior high students. The step-by-step procedure is described in a practical and detailed manner.

Furukawa, J.M. *A cognitive processing capacity model of teaching and studying applied to biology.* Paper presented at the Annual Convention of the International Reading Association, St. Louis, May 1980. (ED 188 159)

Reports on the cognitive processing capacity model of teaching and studying used to determine whether tenth grade students could improve their performance in biology. The twenty-seven students in the experimental group were taught to study information in quantities that matched their CPC and to chunk these quantities together under a heading in a study outline or diagram. In teaching, the same process was used by the teacher of the experimental group. The control group, another biology class of twenty-seven students, continued to be taught as they had been in the past. After completion of two units of biology, the performances of the experimental group were superior to those of the control group.

Georgia State Department of Education. *A reading program for the 70s: Science,* 1976. (ED 132 512)

Offers a detailed guide citing expert opinion and research in relation to science. Specific activities at the elementary, middle, and secondary school levels are discussed in terms of reading skills involved and the science processes stressed.

Holliday, W.G., & Braun, C. Readability of science materials. *Viewpoints in Teaching and Learning,* 1979, *55,* 55-56.

Describes: 1) readability methods used in science education; 2) techniques useful for facilitating reading comprehension; and 3) research concerned with reducing readability load by using different content structures and recognizing relationships between the structure of textual content and memory.

Johnson, L.N. *Guides for teaching secondary students to read in subject areas,* 1980. (ED 195 971)

Provides help for secondary teachers with content area reading instruction. Two pages are specific to science and include: a list of major skills; information on preparing and administering a directed reading activity; a glossary to explain technical terms for the teachers; and appendices containing instructions on preparing a cloze or maze assessment, a structured overview, writing patterns, and mapping techniques.

Kaplan, E.M., & Tuchman, A. Vocabulary strategies belong in the hands of learners. *Journal of Reading*, 1980, *24*, 32-34.

Describes five strategies that foster independent learning of content area vocabulary; 1) prior to the reading, students read titles and headings to anticipate new words they may encounter in the reading; 2) the teacher presents key concept words to the class and elicits synonyms; 3) key vocabulary concept words are listed on the board; the students then have two minutes to write as many synonyms as they can that relate to the content area; 4) the students predict the meanings of the words through context; and 5) students construct a matrix in which words of multiple meanings are written; they predict what the definitions will be prior to reading and check their predictions afterward.

Karahalios, S.M. Using advance organizers to improve comprehension of content textbooks. *Journal of Reading*, 1979, *22*, 706-708.

Defines an advance organizer as a written aid to supplement in an explanatory manner the reading and studying of the text. In this article, seventh graders who read a chapter in a science text using a written handout explaining major concepts performed better on posttests than the group without the handout. Implications for further research are suggested.

Keimig, R.T. *System for integrating reading into content areas* (SIRCA): *An earth science application.* Paper presented at the Annual Convention of the International Reading Association, Anaheim, California, May 1976. (ED 122 214)

Examines a system for integrating reading into the earth science curriculum. It is concluded that student, parent, and teacher reactions to SIRCA have been positive.

Kennedy, K. Determining the reading level of biology textbooks. *American Biology Teacher*, 1979, *41*, 301-303.

Describes use of the Fry Readability Scale in detail.

Kruse, R.M. *A comparative study of the effectiveness of formal and informal teaching in science, math, and social studies*, 1979. (ED 183 394)

Discusses the effectiveness of an instructional program in reading and language development in the content areas of science, social studies, and mathematics in grade two. An experimental group received formally prepared lessons in reading for twenty minutes per day for five weeks each in science, social studies, and mathematics, while the control group did not receive formally prepared lessons. The researcher concluded that formal and informal teaching were equally successful.

Lamb, W.G. Ask a higher-level question, get a higher-level answer. *Science Teacher*, 1976, *43*, 22-23.

Discusses the need for stressing high-level types of questions to improve comprehension. Extensive references are provided for further reading.

Leonard, W.H., & Lowery, L.F. A criterion for biology textbook selection. *American Biology Teacher*, 1976, *38*, 477-479.

Suggests that the style of question presentation should be an issue addressed by those interested in biology textbook selection since it has a considerable effect upon comprehension. An instrument it described: the Textbook Questioning Strategy Assessment Instrument (TQSAI) which categorizes questions within the text by 1) frequency, 2) experience, 3) type, and 4) science process. Directions for using the TQSAI are included.

Ley, T.C., Henry, L.L., & Rowsey, R.E. Eighth graders' performance in reading and computing for science related word problems. *Journal of Reading*, 1979, *23*, 222-228.

Describes a study which hypothesizes that general reading ability, problem-solving reading and thinking skills, and computational skills are related positively to performance in science-related word problems. A math test and word problem test, both specific to science, were administered to two eighth grade classes. The tests included 1) literal comprehension questions, 2) specialized vocabulary questions, 3) recognition of the task to be completed, 4) selection of appropriate solutions, and 5) the actual solution to the problem.

Results suggest that the students were able to compute reasonably well, did understand the literal facts and special vocabulary, and were able to recognize the task to be completed. However, nearly one-third did not choose the appropriate process to solve the problem and an additional seventeen percent did not make an attempt to solve the problem. Implications suggest that students operate ineffectively when analyzing relationships. The authors encourage all content teachers to share in the responsibility for guiding growth of specific reading/thinking skills essential to success in specific content materials. Some suggestions are given.

Lowery, L.F., & Leonard, W.H. Development and method for use of an instrument designed to assess textbook questioning style. *School Science and Mathematics*, 1978, *78*, 393-400.

Suggests that the types, styles, and effectiveness of questions in science texts should be examined prior to selecting an appropriate textbook for classroom use. Suggestions for using the Textbook Questioning Strategy Assessment Instrument (TQSAI) are included.

Manzo, A.V. Three "universal" strategies in content area reading and languaging. *Journal of Reading*, 1980, *24*, 146-149.

Suggests three strategies to help students understand concepts in content area reading: 1) using an oral reading strategy; 2) using the key concept, key terminology, and key question (C/T/Q) strategy; and 3) using the question only strategy.

Miceli, C. Developing a useful model for teaching vocabulary concepts in science. *Science Teacher*, 1975, *42*, 21.

Reports that several junior high school teachers combined efforts and incorporated science vocabulary into their respective content areas. Games were revised and experimental booklets were prepared. The teachers found that retention scores were higher for those students who participated in the experimental program.

Middleton, J.R. *Significant relationships among Louisiana secondary public school biology classes: Readability of biology textbooks, general reading ability, and natural science reading ability.* Doctoral dissertation, Northwestern State University of Louisiana, 1978. *Dissertation Abstracts International*, 1978, *39*, (ED 167 974)

Investigates the possibility of predicting one of the following variables: the readability of biology textbooks, students' natural science reading ability, and students' general reading ability, when only two of the variables are known. Several conclusions were significant, one being that the Fry Readability Graph accurately predicted the readability levels of the biology textbooks.

Morrison, B. *The identification of reading skills essential for learning in seven content areas at postelementary levels,* 1980. (ED 185 536)

Reports on a questionnaire designed to give content area teachers an opportunity to review thirty-five reading/learning skills that are necessary for vocabulary development, the comprehension of written materials, and the efficient use of study time. Over four hundred secondary teachers in seven content areas were asked to indicate the relevancy of each skill for learning their subject matter and their expectations of a student's ability with that skill. Of the thirty-five skills, the following were identified as necessary for learning in the area of science:

Word attack and vocabulary skills: Identifying at sight frequently used words; using clues from the sentence to determine the meaning of an unfamiliar word; using roots, prefixes, and suffixes to determine the meaning of an unfamiliar word; and seeking appropriate meanings for technical words and phrases.

Comprehension Skills: Questioning the relevance of information to a topic, and making use of transitional words, phrases and clauses as bridges to join ideas.

Study skills: Adjusting rate to the purpose for reading; using basic references as needed; formulating questions relevant to the purpose for reading; skimming material for overview; utilizing sources to locate materials; recognizing proper documentation of ideas by an author; following directions; and planning time.

Nelson, J. Readability: Some cautions for the content area teacher. *Journal of Reading,* 1978, *21,* 620-625.

Suggests other factors to consider besides common readability formulas when judging readability of content texts: levels of abstraction, complexity of concepts, figurative language, multiple meanings of technical and scientific vocabulary, and variation in format, to name a few.

Perry, C.M. Questions. *American Biology Teacher,* 1979, *41,* 360-362.

Discusses good questioning techniques for classroom teachers: wait-time after asking questions is encouraged to allow for more comprehensive answers; teachers are encouraged to monitor their own question-asking behavior; and the asking of higher-level questions versus recall-type questions is discussed.

Putnam, L.R. *Skills and techniques useful in developing reading abilities in science,* 1979. (ED 184 089)

Incorporates methods primarily associated with teaching reading as an isolated subject. Recommendations include: determining the student's reading instructional level, matching text material to that level, developing vocabulary through context clues and Latin and Greek roots, and developing main ideas through study outlines.

Ricker, K.S. But can they read it? a look at readability formulas. *Science Teacher,* 1978, *45,* 22-24.

Recognizes several formulas used to assess readability (Fry, FOG, SMOG), with most dealing objectively with the text. However, suggests other factors to be considered when choosing which formula to apply: the text's use, the student's familiarity with the text, vocabulary presentation, writing style, glossing techniques, and the need for teacher adjustment.

Shuman, B.R. Teaching teachers to teach reading in secondary school content classes. *Journal of Reading,* 1978, *22,* 205-211.

Offers useful and practial ideas for all subjects. Recommends use of alphabetizing, cloze procedure to determine readability, a group approach to untangle sentence structure, glossing skills, and teaching techniques for special vocabulary.

Shymansky, J.A., & Yore, L.D. Assessing and using readability of elementary science texts. *School Science and Mathematics*. 1979, *77*, 670-676.
　　　Describes readability methods for science texts and their variability. Teacher strategies to overcome difficulties with text readability are also discussed.

Texas Education Agency. *Strategies for improving reading skills in science*, 1981. (ED 200 955)
　　　Designed particularly with secondary school teachers in mind but applicable to elementary school teachers as well, this publication summarizes research and suggests activities for improving student reading skills in the content area of science. Sections of the publication provide the following information: how to determine student reading levels with the use of informal reading inventories, cloze procedures, and the San Diego Quick Assessment; ways to estimate the reading levels of instructional materials; tips on improving student reading skills; tips on effective note-taking; strategies for test taking, both objective and essay; and questioning techniques that teachers can use to improve student comprehension.

Thelen, J. *Improving reading in science*. Newark, Delaware: International Reading Association, 1976. (ED 116 181)
　　　Suggests that science content and reading processes may be taught simultaneously in the classroom. Six chapters detail and develop this idea. Two appendices include an informal study skills inventory on a physical science textbook and an extensive statement to students about learning to think.

Van Duren, A.E. Improving basic skills in the modified science classroom. *American Biology Teacher*, 1979, *41*, 471-474.
　　　Describes useful techniques for improving the reading and writing skills of poor readers: use of the cloze procedure for text selection, teaching students how to survey the text, allowing student participation in curricular decision-making, encouraging group discussion, and use of positive reinforcement through contracting.

Warren, R.A. Helping poor readers in secondary science. *Science Teacher*, 1975, *42*, 55.
　　　Describes the preparation of audio materials for poor readers. The directions are extremely detailed and practical.

Wright, J.D. *The effect of reduced readability text material on comprehension and biology achievement*. Doctoral dissertation, University of North Carolina at Chapel Hill, 1980. *Dissertation Abstracts International*, 1980, *41*, (ED 197 313)
　　　Investigates the effect on high school students' comprehension and biology achievement of using materials written at a lower readability than that of the assigned biology text. The results were not significant.

Wright, J.D., & Hounshell, P.B. Enhance reading through science. *Science Teacher*, 1978, *45*, 34-36.
　　　Discusses many areas of reading and science: material selection, diagnosis of reading skills, reading skill development, and instructional planning.

Yore, L., & Quinn, K. *Improving the reading of visual materials in intermediate and junior secondary school science*, 1977. (ED 157 004)
　　　Suggests that in helping students to read materials in intermediate level science classes, teachers should first motivate them to read and should set a purpose and a focus for their reading. A postreading discussion should follow each reading task, in order to help students share, integrate, and apply insights obtained from the written materials. Reading science materials involves such tasks as: making measurements; reading graphs, maps, blueprints, star charts, diagrams, and pictures; and decoding statements. Each of these tasks requires specific skills, and instructional techniques may be devised to help students develop these skills.

Science

# Reading in the
# Content Area of Social Studies

Philip Berryhill
*Bald Eagle Area School District*
*Wingate, Pennsylvania*

## Overview

Literature focusing on the application of reading instruction in the social studies consistently identifies the need for an integrated approach between the two areas. The teacher not only must be concerned with what content is to be learned but how and what techniques are necessary in helping the students learn the content.

Mahoney (1977) suggests that most social studies teachers emphasize their responsibility as one of content. "The content comes first with the reading skills subordinate to the nature of the content. In practice, that means that reading is taught if there is time" (p. 2). Traditionally, reading instruction has been isolated as a subject to be taught by the classroom teacher or reading specialist. One problem Levy (1978) notes is that "remedial and developmental aspects of reading have been taught in isolation, with a sublime faith that skills will automatically be applied to reading tasks in all disciplines" to the exclusion of systematic reading instruction in the content areas (p. 18).

Reading instruction in the social studies classroom is often overlooked or avoided for a variety of reasons. "Often, teachers assume that students understand a concept if they can simply read the words in a textbook or use the term in a discussion" (Otero & Moeller, 1977, p. 43). Otero and Moeller further state that some terms may be easy to decode in context, but additional skills are necessary in understanding the concepts and how they apply to other similar issues. Teachers who do not have a background in the skill areas related to the reading process may have difficulty in properly diagnosing students' understanding of content material.

Various researchers identify reading as the most important skill necessary for mastering social studies content. Cassidy (1978) states, "student success in social studies is solidly based on the ability to read to obtain information. Despite this, time is rarely devoted to the actual teaching of reading within the block of time allocated for social studies" (p. 62). Emlyn Jones, as cited in "A Reading Program for the 70s" (Georgia State Department of Education, 1975), identifies reading as the single most important information-gathering skill in the area of social studies in spite of the tremendous growth of instructional aids. Davis (1975) indicates that often it is the student's reading ability which serves as the critical factor in determining a student's success or failure in school. Kerber (1980) regards "the importance of reading as paramount in the social studies; it is the vehicle through which events and concepts come alive" (p. 13).

Teachers in secondary level social science classes have an obligation to meet the needs of pupils, including a wide range of reading abilities. Reading becomes more important as a learning medium at the secondary level. Instructional focus needs to be directed toward the reading demands of the course in relation to the student's abilities to cope with those demands. Dea (1978) provides an estimate by Everhart and Lloyd that over 75 percent of learning at the secondary level is acquired through reading, though very little instruction is given to reinforce basic reading skills. Dea suggests that priorities shift from learning to read in the elementary school to reading to learn in the secondary school. For the disabled reader, the problem becomes increasingly complex due to the progressively more difficult course content.

Davis (1975) cites Aukerman, who suggests that:

> It is safe to estimate that within a world history class at the tenth-grade level, in a class where IQs often range from 85 to 140, and where the average age is 16, there will probably be eight grade levels of reading ability represented in that class. The teacher is confronted with the challenge of teaching these students often with only one textbook and a limited amount of reference material. Thus, since most learning in the secondary school history classroom is through the use of textbooks, reading skills become the "common denominator" of learning in such classrooms (p. 3).

The student needs to develop the reading skills which will enable him to read with understanding the content that is presented in the social studies classroom. In addition, the student is usually required to apply those reading skills outside of the classroom when working independently. Social studies teachers with a limited background in reading require ideas, techniques, and approaches in an attempt to provide functional reading skill instruction for those students.

## Research

Many of the activities in social studies classrooms require students to read and locate main ideas and supporting details. Traditionally, the main idea is thought to be located in the topic sentence at the beginning of a paragraph. Donlan (1980) found that "a recent study of topic sentences in expository prose showed that only 13 percent of the paragraphs of contemporary writers began with topic sentences" (p. 136). Donlan conducted a study involving exercises in locating the main idea in social studies texts with 22 students in his secondary reading class. He found that students generally identified the first sentence in the paragraph as the main idea and there was a general lack of agreement between students as to what the main idea was. Donlan questions, "If teachers find it difficult to locate the main ideas, what about the students?" (p. 136).

Kirkwood and Wolfe (1980) conducted a study involving the cloze test in the areas of language arts and social studies. There were four school districts, including 7,201 students in grades four, seven, and ten, involved in the study. The reading passages were found to be too difficult, especially for students with reading difficulties in the lower grades. Few appropriate materials were found and social studies materials were found to be more difficult than language arts materials.

Rakes and McWilliams (1979) selected 300 subjects at the seventh, eighth, and ninth grade levels in two school districts to participate in a study involving cloze tests and group reading inventories in the area of social studies. The study findings suggest, "properly constructed and administered cloze tests and group reading inventories in social studies can be used to accurately place readers in placement level categories, particularly between frustration and instructional/independent levels" (p. 13). In considering the reading ability requirements of textbooks, teachers should use informal types of reading assessment in addition to standardized test results.

Diem (1980) carried out a study in one Texas school district with secondary social studies teachers to determine the inadequacies in students' reading performance in the area of social studies. The teachers identified the students' inability to handle textbooks and supplementary material as the most serious weakness. Teachers admitted they did not have the preparation to solve the problems, yet they agreed that content mastery in social studies was dependent on the student's ability to comprehend the material.

## Skills

The most common source of learning material in the social studies classroom is the textbook. The readability of social studies textbooks is generally at or above grade level. Lunstrum and Taylor (1978) suggest using the SMOG readability formula for social studies textbooks, particularly when independent reading is required of the students (p. 16).

The reading gap is a comparison between the readability level of the textbook and the student's reading ability. When a large gap exists between the student's ability and the level of the reading content, the teacher should consider alternatives to instruction including a multitext approach (Mahoney, 1977, p. 5).

Blake (1975) suggests that the specific skills required for reading social studies material include:

1. Specialized technical vocabulary development
2. Comprehension skills: besides the more general comprehension such as distinguishing between main ideas and details and drawing conclusions, the following are peculiar to social studies.
   a. cause and effect pattern
   b. comparison and contrast pattern
   c. sequential events pattern
   d. fact vs. opinion pattern
   e. graphic pattern
3. Study skills:
   a. developing purpose for reading
   b. using the textbook—table of contents, index, glossary
   c. organizing information—listening
   d. note taking
   e. developing flexibility in reading rate—skimming and scanning (p. 7)

Cassidy (1978) and others identify a similar list of skills which apply to social studies content. Blake (1975) lists three strategies for developing vocabulary in social studies including context, structure, and game-like activities. Comprehension of social studies content requires all of the comprehension levels outlined in Barrett's Taxonomy of Reading Comprehension and is dependent on the students' understanding and application of concepts and relationships presented. Study skills provide the student with a method of attacking reading assignments with a specific purpose.

Blake (1975) identifies the reading of maps, graphs, and charts as the most specialized type of reading in the social studies due to the decoding and symbol interpretation requirements. Otero and Moeller (1977) advise that map, chart, and graph skills must be learned and student comprehension comes from experiencing and understanding the process of decoding the graphic symbols.

Reading and study skills in the area of social studies include many of the general skills required for reading in all areas, but also some specialized skills. Mastery of technical vocabulary and the interpretation of relationships and concepts are of primary importance in social studies (Georgia State Department of Education, 1975).

Otero and Moeller (1977) contend that in social studies classes students come into contact with many terms and concepts which have little meaning because they are not relevant to their background of experiences. The teacher must give the students prereading background instruction before holding the students responsible for what they are to read. Thelen (1979) points out that "if students have nothing in their prior experiences that is relevant to new material to be read they often attempt to memorize it" (p. 4). Social studies teachers can help to bridge the gap between reading materials and students' backgrounds by providing a variety of material which can be used to illustrate and clarify the terms and concepts presented. The mastery and understanding of terms and concepts in social studies is very important in that students are required to make decisions based on those concepts. For many students, understanding concepts is difficult because they cannot see or relate to the situations where the concepts apply.

In selecting materials and content areas to be studied by the students, teachers should investigate the concept density, sophistication level, vocabulary, ethnic background, historical aspects, geographical relevancy, and available supplementary materials (New York State Education Department, 1975).

Singer and Donlan (1980) identify four levels of knowledge in social studies content: facts, concepts, generalizations, and theories. Further, "all higher learning in social studies is based on factual knowledge. . . .Factual learning by itself has limited value. Facts have to be organized into some type of logical framework" (p. 288). Teaching to provide such a logical framework is necessary in social studies.

## Strategies

Otero and Moeller (1977) propose that "teachers must first identify the abilities of their students and then choose activities that will help students increase their skills at reading and thinking" (p. 10). Initially, in attempting to identify reading abilities and integrate reading instruction into the social studies program, Mahoney (1977) suggests using observation, informal testing, and standardized tests to develop a base of information about the various students' reading abilities. Mahoney adds that developing a base of information is essential for teachers to make "a conscientious effort to help their students improve reading skills," not only in social studies, but in all content areas (p. 3).

In the evaluation of the Salt Lake City Inservice Model (Granite School District, 1975), the conclusions reflect that instructors often assume their students possess the necessary reading skills before they come into their classroom and therefore gear their instruction and assignments accordingly. "This could very easily build failure into a student. A few simple surveys, and then some knowledge on how to use available content to develop skills could greatly benefit the education of potential failing students" (p. 80).

When developing a base of information for predicting students' reading ability in the social sciences, teachers may choose Group Reading Inventories, cloze tests, content inventories, maze tests, and other informal assessment as supplemental diagnostic instruments. Teachers can use the information obtained through informal assessment for grouping and providing instruction to meet individual needs. Barone and Agostino (1979) indicate that standardized test results usually have little instructional value.

Content Inventories and Group Reading Inventories are used by teachers to determine the students' ability to read and function with different areas of the textbook. They provide immediate feedback to the teacher indicating the students' ability to use that specific text in learning content material.

Otero and Moeller (1977) identify the cloze procedure as a "useful method for both the teacher and student in determining to what degree the reader comprehends what is read" (p. 16). Further, Lunstrum and Taylor (1978) relate Feely's recommendation to delete every seventh word rather than every fifth word when the cloze is applied to social studies content. Lunstrum and Taylor compare the maze technique to the cloze procedure, where the deletion of words occurs as often as every fifth word or as rarely as every tenth word. The maze test differs from the cloze in that a multiple choice format is utilized. The maze procedure perhaps causes less apprehension for poor readers and younger children due to the multiple choice response option (Lunstrum & Taylor, 1978, pp. 18-19).

Kratzner and Mannies (1979) explain that not all pupils have the same interest or learn at the same rate; therefore, the wider the range of learning options teachers provide for students, the more likely that each student will learn. A wide range of reading abilities can be accommodated when students have the option of more than one textbook. Teaching library skills helps students use supplementary resource materials that in turn help meet the needs of the wide range of reading abilities within a classroom.

Anderson (1978) provides students with frequent activity in sustained silent reading in the social studies class. Anderson reflects that the teacher and student must view comprehension during the silent reading activity as a series of judgments about the worth of ideas and not remembering and repeating all of the facts in the content read.

Lunstrum and Taylor (1978) suggest a content-centered or functional approach to reading instruction where reading skills are "developed as they are needed in the teaching and learning processes of specific social studies courses" (p. 11). A disadvantage of this approach is that it does not address the reading needs of problem readers in the social studies classes.

Davis (1975) reviews a study involving 64 teachers from 14 school districts, who identify the most effective approaches for teaching reading in social studies as follows:

1. Help students learn the special vocabulary in history and the technical terminology. Explain new words and concepts introduced in new chapters.
2. Be very specific when making assignments. Give students instruction in how to find and use reference material needed to complete assignments.
3. Teach students how to read for main ideas, supporting details, different points of view and identifying causes.
4. Teach students how to use a textbook effectively. Provide knowledge of and practice in using the different parts of the book.
5. Give students specific purposes for reading assignments. Help students acquire skills in locating, using, and evaluating information for specific purposes. (p. 11)

More recently, Gaskins (1981) identified eight areas to be included in the content lesson:

1. The teacher develops both content and process *objectives.*
2. The teacher determines which *vocabulary* terms support or represent major concepts and how they should be introduced.
3. The teacher plans a *motivation* discussion designed to activate students' *prior (background) knowledge* and supply them with further information.
4. The teacher directs the students in *surveying* the material and making *predictions* about what it contains.
5. The teacher guides the students, through questioning techniques, in setting *purposes for* their *reading.*
6. The teacher designs a study guide to help students through *guided reading* of content material.
7. The teacher provides meaningful opportunities every day for students to *synthesize and reorganize* the important information and concepts they are learning.
8. The teacher develops a plan for helping the students relate the content and concepts studied to the world in which they live.

This is an outline very much like a Directed Reading Activity, but applies to a reading selection from a content lesson.

## Conclusion

Reading skill deficiences are commonly identified as the major obstacle to students' understanding and mastering social studies content. "The student who has a definite purpose for reading a selection will read it with greater understanding than if he has no other direction than a command to get the job done" (Georgia State Department of Education, 1975, p. 8). Unfortunately, many pupils do not possess the reading skills to read the required materials.

The teacher must be aware of the students' abilities and adjust instruction and assignments accordingly. Textbook readabilities, group reading inventories, content inventories, cloze tests, maze tests, and standardized tests all provide diagnostic information for the teacher. The results obtained from these analytical instruments must be interpreted and used by the teacher in the development of instruction consistent with the needs of individuals and groups of students.

Kerber (1980) advocates the use of social studies trade books and indicates that one way of keeping up with new trade books in social studies is by sending for the annual list "Notable Children's Trade Books in the Field of Social Studies," from the Children's Book Council, 67 Irving Place, New York, New York 10003. The trade books may be used as a supplement and means of motivation in the regular social studies program.

Barone and Agostino (1979) believe indiscriminate "cookbook" approaches to improving reading in social studies may have undesirable side effects. Teachers will be reluctant to spend instructional time on reading techniques where immediate results are not evident. Students will learn that the activities bear little relationship to the real world of social studies unless the teacher helps them develop that relationship. Barone and Agostino make three suggestions for successfully incorporating reading skills into the social studies classroom.

1. Ask "What reading abilities and attitudes do my students possess?"
2. Ask "What reading demands are required by the textbooks and materials used?"
3. Ask "How can I make the appropriate 'instructional match' linking a student's reading skills and attitudes with the appropriate materials and media?" (p. 4)

Social studies teachers may resist the idea of teaching reading skills as an integrated approach to content instruction because they are not familiar with reading methods. Reading personnel can help the content teacher develop an understanding of the feasibility and value of addressing reading skill development in the social studies classroom. Perhaps only a few skills should be introduced periodically in an attempt to avoid overwhelming the content teacher.

The social studies teacher who realizes the need for reading skill emphasis should be provided with guidance and background information, including practical suggestions and approaches which can be implemented in the classroom. Reading personnel in a school system should serve as resource persons in providing suggestions and structure for reading skill application in the social studies and other content area classrooms. Reading specialists may provide students with follow up activities which complement and reinforce the skill areas required for functioning in social studies.

Teacher attitude toward reading instruction in the content area can have a major effect on the success of reading skill application. An initial concern in developing content area reading instruction must be developing positive teacher attitudes toward implementation of the program. Teachers need to feel comfortable with the skills they are teaching before they accept the responsibility for implementing unfamiliar techniques. When teachers have a weak background in the area of reading, they will need step-by-step guidance in dealing with reading skill instruction in their content subjects. Teachers will have different levels of readiness in accepting reading skill development as a method of improving the learning skills of students in the content classroom.

Just as teachers provide for students' individual differences, content reading emphasis must be prepared to provide for teachers' individual differences. Factors including motivation, understanding, experiential background, attitudes, skills, and readiness apply to content teachers as well as to the effectiveness of instruction in the content classroom.

Teachers need to be aware that reading skill emphasis in the content area can make a difference in providing students with an opportunity to learn content. Teacher also must have a positive attitude toward integrating reading instruction as a supplement to content instruction. To be effective, teachers need to have a commitment to making content reading instruction a consistent part of their program.

# Annotated Bibliography for
# Reading in Social Studies

Anderson, J., et al..*Jeremiah E. Burke high school multicultural, multiethnic reading skills curriculum guide*. Portsmouth, New Hampshire: New England Teachers Corps Network, 1978. (ED 185 521)

Draws materials from a variety of sources to help teachers develop student reading skills while indirectly exposing students to the customs, vocabularies, and histories of various ethnic groups and cultures. Activities are suggested for a variety of reading skills including real life and newspaper reading skills.

Barone, W.P., & Agostino, V.R. *Reading competence in social studies*, 1979. (ED 186 329)

Suggests that reading instruction is being incorporated as a natural part of the social studies curriculum because of the emphasis which is being placed on basic skills. Social studies teachers are encouraged to develop a systematic and deliberate approach to reading instruction in their classrooms. The paper suggests that the total class is first tested at the macro level using the cloze technique. For students who demonstrate an acceptable level, testing is ended. Students not screened out at this level are tested using other diagnostic techniques, including Content Reading Inventories in Social Studies. The feeling is that many standardized tests have little instructional value.

Beyer, B.K. Teaching basics in social studies. *Social Education*, 1977, *41*, 96-104.

Suggests techniques for integrating reading activities into the social studies lesson on a regular basis.

Blake, S. *Teaching reading skills through social studies and science materials*. Brooklyn: New York City Board of Education, Division of High Schools, 1975. (ED 123 564)

Attempts to assist the reading teacher toward a fuller understanding of the processes and procedures applicable to the teaching of reading using social studies and science materials. The manual provides an overview, a list of teaching techniques for the various reading skills, and model lessons.

Cassidy, J. Putting the "first r" in social studies. *Teacher*, 1978, *95*, 62-64.

States that success in social studies is based on student ability to read to obtain information. In Project CARE, social studies activities are generally keyed to reinforce specific objectives in five areas: vocabulary, map/graph skills, recognizing propaganda, previewing, and study skills.

Cornbleth, C. Using questions in social studies. Arlington, Virginia: National Council for the Social Studies, 1977.

Points out that questions help to determine how and what students learn. Social studies questions are divided into six types: personal belief/experience, memory, comprehension, creative expression, judgment, and followup. Questioning strategies of each type are explained in detail.

Davis, E.D. *Selected secondary school history teachers' suggestions for teaching effectively the special reading skills needed in the study of history*. Southern Methodist University, 1975. (ED 120 680)

Suggests that in order to help students master special skills needed for effective reading, the teacher must be aware of the students' skill abilities and needs. Sixty-four experienced history teachers, trained in the teaching of reading, suggest effective methods for other teachers in the social studies area to consider.

Dea, W.A. *The relationships between vocabulary recognition and higher chapter test scores in United States history classes.* Master's thesis, Whittier College, 1978. (ED 159 595)

In the study, instruction varied between use and nonuse of vocabulary recognition materials for different difficult words to study the possible effect of such materials on test scores. The study's conclusion that vocabulary recognition helps to improve content reading implies that teachers should investigate the reading levels of students and the textbook, followed by attempts to reconcile reading level differences through an emphasis on the difficult vocabulary within the text.

Diem, R.A. *An analysis of a staff development training program in reading and social studies.* Washington, D.C.: Office of Education, 1980. (ED 182 221)

Describes a three year staff development program in reading and social studies in San Antonio, Texas. Teachers felt their students could not master social studies materials because they could not read them. To attack this problem, a staff development program that would train teachers in functional reading skills was devised and implemented. Results of the project indicated: 1) that student performance in functional reading skills can be increased by training teachers in these skills; 2) a developmental model of inservice training provides a successful design in which teachers can work; and 3) intensive content methodology instruction is needed beyond the basic preservice courses now in effect.

Dolgin, A.B. How to match reading materials to student reading levels: Fry's graph and the diagnostic survey. *Social Studies*, 1975, *66*, 249-452.

Advises social studies teachers to be sensitive to the variability in students' reading abilities. The Fry Graph and diagnostic survey are suggested as basic instruments in identifying the readability levels of materials and individual students' reading levels.

Donlan, D. Locating main ideas in history textbooks. *Journal of Reading*, 1980, *24*, 135-140.

Traditionally main ideas are considered to be included in the topic sentence which usually is thought to be located at the beginning of the paragraph. Donlan states that the main idea can appear anywhere in a paragraph and perhaps may not appear at all. Before teachers can help students locate the main ideas they need to know what the main ideas are themselves. Locating the main idea through critical reading can be a difficult task for teachers as well as students.

Duscher, R. How to help social science students read better. *Social Studies*, 1975, *66*, 258-261.

The integration of reading instruction into social studies can aid students in using class material more effectively. The effective social studies teacher will likely be confronted with the task of providing for individual students' differences in reading abilities.

Feely, T.M., Jr. How to match reading materials to student reading levels: II. The cloze and the maze. *Social Studies*, 1975, *66*, 252-258.

The cloze and maze techniques are relatively easy to administer and score and may be used to match reading levels of materials and students. Seven characteristics are utilized in a comparison between the cloze and maze techniques.

Gaskins, I.W. Reading for learning: Going beyond basals in the elementary grades. *Reading Teacher*, 1981, *35*, 323-328.

Students need teacher guidance in reading content material. Social studies often creates special difficulties for students due to unfamiliar matters, usually remote in time and place, in addition to the high concept density of the materials. This article includes eight areas to consider in the planning of a content lession.

Georgia State Department of Education. *A reading program for the 70s: Social studies and reading*. Atlanta, Georgia: Division of Curriculum Development, 1975 (ED 105 408)

    Offers a plan to help social studies teachers develop the competencies they will need to teach students to read social studies materials in kindergarten through grade twelve. A sample unit and suggested evaluation techniques illustrate the use of many materials at varied reading levels. Classroom organizational patterns that will help the teacher to individualize instruction are suggested. Several techniques useful for determining student reading levels and readability levels of social studies materials are presented.

Granite School District. *An interdisciplinary inservice model for teaching reading in the content areas: Grades 7-9*. Salt Lake City, Utah, 1975. (ED 122 223)

    Describes the development of an integrated approach to teaching content reading skills to teachers. This document contains a copy of the inservice model, an evaluation of the project, and copies of the materials developed for use in each specific skill area.

Hughey, R.M., & Fillmer, H.T. Reading inventory for secondary school social studies teachers: How do you rate? *Social Education*, 1980, *44*, 14-20.

    Presents a 54-item reading inventory with answer key and rating scale for secondary school social studies teachers.

Johnson, R.E., & Vardian, E.B. Reading, readability, and social studies. *Reading Teacher*, 1973, 483-488.

    Suggests that readability formulas produce varied results; therefore, more than one readability formula should be used when determining the readability of textbooks. Readability formulas applied to social studies textbooks typically show that those textbooks are written on or above grade level which creates difficulty for the slow or low achieving child.

Kerber, J.E. *Special feature: Children's literature*. Ohio Council, International Reading Association, 1980. (ED 192 268)

    Focuses on the use of children's literature in all areas of the curriculum. Discusses change in the social studies and offers teaching methods that stimulate children's thinking about historical and current events.

Kirkwood, K.J., & Wolfe, R.G. *Matching students and reading materials: A cloze procedure method for assessing the reading ability of students and the readability of textual material*. Toronto: Ontario Ministry of Education, 1980. (ED 195 928)

    Involves the use of open-ended cloze testing to establish a criterion for the utility of content reading passages for students in grades four, seven, and ten in the area of social studies. Passages were selected from books, novels, and textbooks required in the courses. Most reading passages were too difficult for most of the students, especially students at the lower end of the reading ability scale. In the lower grades, there were few appropriate materials for the students' reading ability.

Kratzer, R.R., & Mannies, N. Building responsibility and reading skills in the social studies classroom. *Journal of Reading*, 1979, *22*, 502-505./

    Points out that pupils differ from one another in many ways and the more learning options a teacher provides for a class, the more likely that each pupil will learn. A program including four phases—diagnosis, instruction, practice, and application—was developed around effective use of library research skills at the middle school level.

Levy, J.M., et. al.. *Helping students improve reading skills in selected content areas.* Nova University, Practicum Report, 1978. (ED 157 046)

    Reports on 15 secondary teachers who integrated desired teaching strategies with their ongoing instruction of subject content. Test results and evaluation indicated that content area teachers can make a significant contribution to helping students improve their reading skills.

Lundstum, J.P. Reading in the social studies: A preliminary analysis of recent research, *Social Education*, 1976, *40*, 10-18.

    Suggests that social studies teachers should be given formal instruction in how to incorporate reading instruction as an integrated part of the social studies program.

Lunstrum, J.P., & Irvin, J.L. Integration of basic skills into social studies content. *Social Education*, 1981, *45*, 169-177.

    Provides a systematic study guide model which includes strategies for integrating reading skill development with social studies content. The basic model is developed around the content of "The Last March."

Lunstrum, J.P., & Taylor, B.L. *Teaching reading in the social studies.* Newark, Delaware: International Reading Association, 1978. (ED 157 008)

    Presents approaches to improving students' skills in reading social studies materials. Three problem areas are included: matching pupil reading abilities and instructional materials, providing motivation to read in social studies classes, and improving comprehension in the reading of social studies. Within each problem area, selected strategies, procedures, and resources are identified and described in addition to detailed suggested activities.

Mahoney, J.E. *Improving reading skills in social studies.* Arlington, Virginia: National Council for the Social Studies, 1977. (ED 139 724)

    Suggests some practical ways to improve reading skills in social studies classes without sacrificing content objectives and goals. Effective teaching techniques to improve content reading are discussed. It is emphasized that social studies teachers are the best suited to teach reading skills in their own subject field.

New York State Education Department. *Extending high school equivalency reading skills: Science, social studies, mathematics.* Albany, New York: Bureau of Continuing Education Curriculum Development, 1975. (ED 116 137)

    Reinforces reading skills for interpreting exercises in the social studies test sections of the General Education Development (GED) Test. This is designed as a curriculum supplement with practice examples included.

Otero, G.G., Jr., & Moeller, C. *Teaching reading in the social studies: A global approach, skill series volume one.* Denver, Colorado: Center for Teaching International Relations, University of Denver, 1977. (ED 143 562)

    Presents an activity supplement for social studies teachers, grades 6-12, with a global focus. Teachers are provided with basic tools to use in assessing social studies materials. There are nine chapters, each of which contains a general introduction followed by teaching activities for which objectives, grade level, time, materials, and procedures are specified.

Price, R.D. Teaching reading is not the job of the social studies teacher. *Social Education*, 1978, *42*, 312-315.

    Observes that student success in the area of social studies has traditionally been dependent on ability to read the assigned material. Five reasons are provided in support of the view that teaching reading through social studies is not feasible beyond the primary grades.

*Berryhill*

Rakes, T.A., & McWilliams, L.J. *A comparison of performance on cloze in grades seven, eight, and nine.* Paper presented at the annual meeting of the College of Reading Association, Boston, November 1979. (ED 186 854)

 Reports on student participation in a comparative study of performance on social studies cloze tests, social studies group reading inventories, and the Gates-MacGinitie, Survey E, standardized reading test. Cloze tests and GRIS constructed from social studies materials differentiated independent, instructional, and frustration level readers. The study concluded that teachers concerned with student textbook reading ability should try informal types of reading assessment in addition to standardized reading achievement tests.

Schneider, D.O., & Brown, M.J.M. Helping students study and comprehend their social studies textbooks. *Social Education*, 1980, *44*, 105-112.

 Suggests strategies and activities for developing structured overviews and study guides as a means for organizing content. Illustrations and descriptions are provided for each of three emphasized reading phases: Prereading, Reading, and Postreading.

Singer, H., & Donlan, D. *Reading and learning from text.* Boston: Little, Brown, 1980, 281-314.

 The text overview includes: social studies as an academic discipline, levels of thought and processes, types of social studies texts and strategies in dealing with those texts, as they relate to social studies content.

Solovy, D.A. The teaching of reading in social studies. *Social Studies*, 1975, *66*, 80-82.

 Observes that the social studies teacher is responsible for identifying students' reading abilities and meeting their needs. Techniques are suggested for integrating reading acitivities into social studies lessons on a regular basis.

Standal, T.C. How to use readability formulas more effectively. *Social Education*, 1981, *45*, 181-186.

 Identifies readability formulas as complex measures; however, they exclude such important factors as the effects of motivation background experiences and concept complexity. Though readability formulas have limitations, they provide a general indicator of the difficulty level of materials for teachers. The teachers, on the other hand, must be aware of the variables which readability formulas do not take into account.

Taylor, B.L. Teaching reading is part of the social studies teacher's job. *Social Education*, 1978, *42*, 312-315.

 Notes that students in social studies classes generally are taught only those skills necessary to master the content of the materials. Social studies teachers, through the cooperation and assistance of reading teachers, can use their material as a vehicle for reading instruction.

Thelen, J.N. *Role of prereading in content learning.* Paper presented at the annual meeting, West Virginia University Reading Center, June 1979. (ED 174 962)

 Suggests that teachers should provide prereading techniques designed to provide experiences relevant to new concepts to be learned by students. Content reading problems stem from comprehension problems due to lack of relevant background knowledge. Teachers should be the primary source of information; textbooks should be used to reinforce social studies concepts which have been developed previously.

Turner, T.N. Question games for social studies. *Social Education*, 1981, *45*, 169-177.

 Includes thirteen games designed from television games as examples of activities to motivate students. Students participate in both the asking and answering of questions.

Tyo, J. An alternative for poor readers in social science. *Social Education*, 1980, *44*, 309-310.

Reports that poor readers who listened to the social studies assignments read on a tape scored significantly higher on a social studies cloze test than students confined to print alone. Results of this study indicate that the use of a listening approach appeared to facilitate poor readers' comprehension.

## Texts in the Field of Content Area Reading

Allington, R., & Strange, M. *Learning through reading in the content areas.* Lexington, Massachusetts: D.C. Heath, 1980, 258 pp., paper.

Askov, E.N., & Kamm, K. *Study skills in content areas.* Boston: Allyn and Bacon, 1982, 212 pp., paper.

Aukerman, R.C. *Reading in the secondary school classroom.* New York: McGraw-Hill, 1972.

Aulls, M.W. *Developmental and remedial reading in the middle grades.* Boston: Allyn & Bacon, 1978, abridged edition, 366 pp., paper.

Brunner, J.F., & Campbell, J.J. *Participating in secondary reading: A practical approach.* Englewood Cliffs, New Jersey: Prentice—Hall, 1978, 228 pp.

Burmeister, L.E. *Reading strategies for secondary school teachers* (2nd ed.). Reading, Massachusetts: Addison-Wesley, 1978, 398 pp.

Burron, A., & Claybaugh, A.L. *Using reading to teach subject matter: Fundamentals for content teachers.* Columbus, Ohio: Charles E. Merrill, 1974, 120 pp., paper.

Cunningham, J.W., Cunningham, P.M., & Arthur, S.V. *Middle and secondary school reading.* New York: Longman, 1981, 363 pp., paper.

Dillner, M.H., & Olson, J.P. *Personalizing reading instruction in middle, junior, and senior high schools, utilizing a competencey based instructional system.* New York: Macmillan, 1977, 544 pp., paper.

Dishner, E.K., Bean, T.W., & Readence, J.E. *Reading in the content areas: Improving classroom instruction.* Dubuque, Iowa: Kendall/Hunt, 1981, 288 pp., paper.

Dupuis, M.M., & Askov, E.N. *Content area reading: An individualized approach.* Englewood Cliffs, New Jersey: Prentice-Hall, 1982, 382 pp.

Estes, T.H., & Vaughan, J.L., Jr. *Reading and learning in the content classroom: Diagnostic and instructional strategies.* Boston: Allyn & Bacon, 1978. Full text casebound; abridged edition paper, 277 pp.

Forgan, H.W., & Mangrum, C.T. *Teaching content area reading skills: A modular preservice and inservice program* (2nd ed.). Columbus, Ohio: Charles E. Merrill, 1981, 314 pp., paper.

Hafner, L.E. *Developmental reading in middle and secondary schools: Foundations, strategies, and skills for teaching.* New York: Macmillan, 1977, 583 pp.

Hafner, L.E. *Improving reading in middle and secondary schools: Selected readings* (2nd ed.). New York: Macmillan, 1974, 475 pp., paper.

Herber, H.L. *Teaching reading in content areas* (2nd. ed.). Englewood Cliffs, New Jersey: Prentice-Hall, 1978, 316 pp.

Hill, W.R. *Secondary school reading: Process, program, procedure.* Boston: Allyn & Bacon, 1979, 430 pp.

Karlin, R. *Teaching reading in high school* (2nd ed.). Indianapolis: Bobbs-Merrill, 1972, 375 pp.

Lamberg, W., & Lamb, C.E. *Reading instruction in the content areas.* Chicago: Rand McNally, 1980, 412 pp.

Manning, M.M., & Manning, G.L. *Reading instruction in the middle school.* Washington, D.C.: National Education Association, 1979, 95 pp., paper.

Miller, W.H. *Teaching reading in the secondary school.* Springfield, Illinois: Charles C. Thomas, 1974, 520 pp.

Olson, A., & Ames, W. *Teaching reading skills in secondary schools.* Scranton, Pennsylvania: Intext Educational, 1972.

Readence, J.E., Bean, T.W., & Baldwin, R.S. *Content area reading: An integrated approach.* Dubuque, Iowa: Kendall/Hunt, 1981, 233 pp.

Robinson, H.A. *Teaching reading and study strategies: The content areas.* (2nd ed.). Boston: Allyn & Bacon, 1978, 372 pp.

Roe, B.D., Stoodt, B.D., & Burns, P.C. *Reading instruction in the secondary schools* (rev. ed.). Chicago: Rand McNally, 1978, 437 pp.

Shepherd, D.L. *Comprehensive high school reading methods.* (3rd ed.). Columbus, Ohio: Charles E. Merrill, 1982, 400 pp.

Singer, H., & Donlan, D. *Reading and learning from text.* Boston: Little, Brown, 1980.

Smith, C.B., & Elliott, P.G. *Reading activities for middle and secondary schools: A handbook for teachers.* New York: Holt, Rinehart and Winston, 1979, 226 pp., paper.

Smith, C.B., Smith, S.L., & Mikulecky, L. *Teaching reading in secondary school content subjects: A bookthinking process.* New York: Holt, Rinehart and Winston, 1978, 466 pp.

Smith, R.J., & Barrett, T.C. *Teaching reading in the middle grades* (2nd ed.). Reading, Massachusetts: Addison-Wesley, 1979, 228 pp., paper.

Thomas, E.L., & Robinson, H.A. *Improving reading in every class: A sourcebook for teachers* (2nd ed.). Boston: Allyn & Bacon, 1982. Full text, 431 pp. casebound; abridged edition, 337 pp., paper.

Tonjes, M.J., & Zintz, M.V. *Teaching reading/thinking/study skills in content classrooms.* Dubuque, Iowa: William C. Brown, 1981, 436 pp., paper.

Vacca, R.T. *Content area reading.* Boston: Little, Brown, 1981, 392 pp.

Social Studies